TRUTHSPEAK

TRUTHSPEAK

**The True Meaning of Five Key Christian Words
Distorted Through Religious Newspeak**

Michael D. Halsey

Grace Gospel Press
Milwaukee, Wisconsin

Truthspeak: The True Meaning of Five Key Christian Words Distorted Through Religious Newspeak
©2010 Michael D. Halsey

ISBN: 978-0-9799637-2-8

Library of Congress Control Number: 2010939651

GGP

Grace Gospel Press
10328 W. Oklahoma Ave.
Milwaukee, WI 53227
U.S.A.
www.gracegospelpress.com

Printed in the United States of America

To my parents, James and Mollie Halsey,
a gift of God's grace to me,
a gift which has never stopped giving.

ACKNOWLEDGMENTS

God has graciously brought many people into my life people to whom I will always be both grateful and indebted.

It was from Mrs. R. P. Johnson, my high school Latin teacher for three years, that I first heard the maxim, "Little minds discuss people. Mediocre minds discuss events. Great minds discuss ideas." Dr. Peder Christiansen, my Latin and Greek professor at Texas Tech University for 177 class periods (I missed one, attending 176), brought that adage into his always interesting and never a dull moment classroom as we discussed the great ideas contained in the words and works of the poets and politicians of ancient Greece and Rome. My desire has always been to be a teacher cut from the same pedagogical cloth as they.

I am also indebted to the faculty of thirteen from 1965-1969 at Dallas Theological Seminary, each making their own unique contributions to build a solid, consistent, grace-oriented theology into my life.

Outside academia, God has brought into my orbit many gracious believers such as Hugh Akin, a source of continual encouragement. He has been one of those "faithful Achates" in my life to whom I will always be grateful.

As someone observed, "A person can't have too many friends," and I appreciate the co-laborers in grace whom I've known throughout the years: Pete and Evelyn Hogue, Lora Canter, and Ralph and Gwen Spaugh, whose hearth and hearts were always open to me and mine. The friends and members of County Line Church, Hampton, GA, also deserve special mention for allowing me to labor in their vineyard; these pages don't contain the space I would need to express my love and gratitude to them. Such an "Achates List" could go on and on.

I'm also indebted to my wife Mary who encouraged me to sit at the computer and think through my fingers in order to write *Truthspeak*. Her encouragement has been "far above rubies."

Eternity will tell the names of others who rightfully deserve to be mentioned for shaping my life. In regard to the ones named and unnamed I can only say, "Thank you" to them and for them to God.

CONTENTS

PREFACE

WORDS ARE THE DRESS
OF THOUGHT

L ord Chesterfield said those words, and he continued,
"which should no more be presented in rags, tatters,
and dirt, than your person should." Chesterfield was
arguing for precision and clarity of language.

George Orwell wrote a novel in which the government
of Oceania engaged in "dressing thought" by creating
"Newspeak," the language of that nation in 1984.

Newspeak was nefarious with malicious intent; the
government created it to limit the thinking and range
of thought of its citizens in order to control them. "Big
Brother" knew that without words, thinking would be
impossible and he knew that if he changed the meanings of words, if he loaded foreign concepts into words,
and if he changed the definitions of words, then he had
yet another tool in his arsenal of totalitarian control.
Words are like bread; they are food for the mind; but
with no words, there is no food for thought.

To understand the importance of definitions, consider Aristotle who defined the human being by saying,
"Man is a thinking animal." Is that a human being? Or

is the definition of man what we read in Genesis 1:26-27, a special creation of God, made in the image and likeness of God, unique and separate from angels, animals, and plants? Abortion, euthanasia, and genocide hinge on which of those definitions, animal or image, powerful people choose.

"Peace" flows from the mouth of the communist as it does from the American statesman, politician, and capitalist. All use the same word, but all are not on the same page of Webster's dictionary. As Solange Hertz writes, "The orthodox definition of peace is the tranquility of order, but in communist lingo peace is merely the freedom to carry on the dialectical conflict. In other words, peace is actually war, the establishment of permanent, self-perpetuating revolution."

Newspeak for peace: "Peace is war."

When the communist insists that he longs for "peace," the once-fearful capitalist is relieved, thinking he's found a friend with a common purpose, when, in fact, he is dealing with the opposite. This is unknown to him because Newspeak has hidden the true intent of the communist.

If the government of Oceania had decided to initiate a health care reform initiative and found that its citizens were on the verge of rebellion against it, they could quell the seditious fires by changing the terminology to "health *insurance* reform." Over time, once "health care reform" was forgotten, the people could only think of and debate "health insurance reform."

When Oceania invented Newspeak, it not only redefined words, but it only allowed words to be used in restricted ways. For example, "free" was in their lexicon, but Big Brother restricted its usage to such things as, "My dog is free from fleas." Oceania never permitted the word "free" to be used in reference to a person's being politically free from Big Brother.

Therefore, to be politically free was unthinkable because there were no words in which to dress the thought and if there are no words in which to dress the thought, the thought is inexpressible. Result: control.

What if the great words of the Bible have been tampered with? What if the definitions of five important Bible words have been changed? What if they're being forced to carry baggage foreign to them? There are five words we hear all the time in churches and five words we read constantly in Christian books, but what if they have been so tampered with that whenever we hear them or read them, we are unable to think about, understand, and most important of all, believe what they are biblically communicating to us?

What if, because of the tampering, something alien has been introduced into the gospel and because of the tampering, Christianity must take its place as only one more religion in the world's pantheon of religions, one which has been changed into works? What if by such interference, people are immersed in a works system of salvation and they can't see it because the changing of the words will not allow them to see it? What if they cannot chew on the bread of life because the "bread" has been changed to straw? What if, because of this immersion into works, one day they will hear, "Depart from Me, I never knew you" (Matthew 7:23)?

I want to show you that five important words in Christianity, "grace," "finished," "repentance," "believe," and "justified" have been ripped from their biblical meanings, and been dressed so that biblically alien concepts have been loaded into them, with the result that their meanings have been misunderstood, and that, by such adjustments, Bible words with Bible definitions have been lost. I want to show you that Bible words are coming to us in different clothes, not the dress of the New Testament authors.

You will find each chapter title written in Newspeak, thereby showing the new dress for the old doctrines and, clothed in Newspeak, the Bible words with the Bible definitions are unrecognizable.

What we have lost, we need to reclaim.

CHAPTER ONE

NEWSPEAK: "GRACE IS WORKS"

Grace is the context of the Bible, the grid through which we read the story of God's interaction with the human race. Grace is the lens through which we view man's cooperation or lack thereof with the revelation of God.

Jesus Christ came "full of *grace* and truth." Paul begins his epistles with the greeting, "*Grace* and peace." To Titus he writes, "*Grace* teaches us . . ." In Romans we read, "We were justified freely by His *grace*." In Ephesians 2:8-9, we are saved "by *grace* and not of works." In Galatians we learn that we ruin God's grace if we mix works with it because, if salvation is by one tiny work, grace gets an infection and dies an instant death.

For the Bible-believing Christian, grace is in his heart, it's in his soul, and it'll be his breath should he grow old.

GRACE DEFINED

Grace is "unmerited favor," and by "unmerited" we mean UNMERITED, as in "undeserved," "unearned."

As L. S. Chafer wrote, "Pure grace is neither treating a person as he deserves, nor treating a person better than he deserves, but treating a person without the slightest reference to what he deserves."

Chafer also wrote on the importance of getting the meaning of grace right: "The exact and discriminate meaning of the word *grace* should be crystal clear to every child of God. With such insight only can he feed his own soul on the inexhaustible riches which it unfolds, and with such understanding only can he be enabled clearly to pass on to others its marvelous, transforming theme . . . *Grace* means pure unrecompensed kindness and favor. What is done in grace is done graciously. From this exact meaning there can be no departure; otherwise grace ceases to be grace."

GRACE VISUALIZED

To give us a word picture of grace, Paul writes that it's like a gift, which, by its very nature is free or it's no gift. To emphasize salvation's "giftness," Paul pens "free" before "gift." To be a gift, it must come stringless; no obligations attached. John, to show that God offers salvation without obligations and oblations, records Jesus as telling a woman, "If you knew the gift of God . . . you would have asked . . . and He would have *given* you living water." When Jesus offers salvation, He says it's something "given." He doesn't say, ". . . and He would have told you how to earn living water."

ANCIENT GRACE

In the first book of the Bible, we see free grace when we read, "And Abraham believed God and it was counted to him for righteousness." (Genesis 15:6) The righteousness came upon the belief.

Earlier in the book, God had announced the good news of the gift, promising that the Seed of the Woman would come and defeat Satan and what he had done in the Fall (Genesis 3:15). Sixty-five books, twenty chapters, sixteen verses, and fourteen hundred years later, God nails the point: "Whoever is thirsty, let him come; and whoever wishes, let him take the free gift of the water of life" (Revelation 22:17). From cover to cover, salvation is a gift, a free one.

A gift means no promises, nor performances, no vows nor votive candles, no surrendering of the soul, nor cost, nor commitments made to the giver. If there are any of those things, then whatever is offered isn't a gift, it's an exchange and an exchange is never a condition for salvation because to make an exchange takes it out of the gift category. I have yet to open a Christmas or birthday present and find a bill inside. If the package contains a billing statement, it's no gift.

UNIQUE GRACE

Grace means that Christianity doesn't stand in a line with the world's religions waiting its turn to tell us what things we're supposed to do, what rules, regulations, ordinances, liturgies, and commands we're to keep to get God to like us, be impressed with us, and then, when we've performed enough, let us into His heaven. Nor does Christianity stand in a line with the religions of the world telling us what sins we're to give up or be willing to give up to find grace and be given the gift of life. Grace has no scales by which man's deeds, good and bad, are held in the balance and pronounced "good enough" or "wanting."

Grace holds no hoops through which we're to jump because when it comes to salvation, there is neither "how high," nor "how far." If there were, the leap would be impossible because it must be a perfect jump; it would be a leap too high and too far, since a holy God must demand a perfect leap or lose His own holiness, a holiness drowned in compromise.

MIXED GRACE

What the Bible is presenting conceptually and explicitly is that grace and works are distinct, antithetical one to the other. So different are the two systems, that no work, no good deed can be introduced into grace without changing grace into works. It doesn't work the other way either; grace cannot be mixed with works; the reason is obvious, the result is the same. Salvation is not our doing our part and God's supplying the rest of the merits we need.

Because of what grace is, it's wrong to believe we're to do what we can, all we can, and to do that good for as long as we can, then, God mixes grace with what we've done.

This is akin to our entrance into heaven coming in whatever high-octane mixture we need of works fuel and grace fuel, propelling us onward and upward to heaven. Grace is not an ad hoc additive to performance petrol to give us that needed booster rocket to glory. It is either all of grace or it is not.

This admixture of human octane and grace is an old heresy; we come across it in church history in the fourth and fifth centuries as delineated by Pelagius (ca. 350-ca. 418) whose influence continues today. He taught that human beings have a natural capacity to reject evil and seek God; that Christ's admonition, "Be ye perfect," presupposes this capacity, and that grace is the natural ability given by God to seek and to serve God. Pelagius rejected the doctrine of original sin, believing that children are born innocent of the sin of Adam. Baptism ceased to be interpreted as a regenerative sacrament. Pelagius challenged the very function of the church, claiming that the law as well as the gospel can lead one to heaven and that pagans had been able to enter heaven by virtue of their moral actions before the coming of Christ.

Pelagius taught that man's works form either all (as in the case of pagans before the coming of Christ) or part of the octane of salvation. His heresy persists. I've heard a Protestant pastor, influenced knowingly or unknowingly by Pelagius, tell his people, "Salvation is 90% God and 10% you," in contrast to Jonah who said, "Salvation is of the Lord." The Bible knows nothing of a percentage salvation. Yet the same pastor could read and recite Ephesians 2:8-9 and not see the clash between his percentage gospel which Paul declares is "no gospel" in Galatians 1, and the gospel of grace.

Grace is a divine and revolutionary intervention of God into the human race. This intervention is what gives Christianity its uniqueness—salvation by 100% pure grace is not an idea anyone could originate. No religion has ever come up with such an idea. The human mind, fallen and curved in on itself, is only capable of originating one endless works system after another and each works system stands opposed and actively hostile to grace. Paul illustrates the difference in the two systems and the hostility of works to grace by using the analogy of Ishmael's persecution and hatred of Isaac. Ishmael represents works; Isaac represents grace. So incompatible were the two, Ishmael had to go. There can be no treaty between works and grace, no peace talks to engineer a solution.

Grace allows for no works to earn salvation and less than none to keep it. Paul showed that grace was separate from works by writing, "And if by grace, then it is no longer by works; if it were, grace would no longer be grace." (Romans 11:6)

NEWSPEAK: GRACE IS WORKS

But grace has been tampered with. "Grace" is in the lexicon of Newspeak and has been for a long, long time. In Newspeak, grace is no longer grace with the Bible's definition.

Early in church history, there were people from "Oceania" who began to meddle with grace and in the tampering, altered it. The same five letters are present, accounted for, and in the same order, "g-r-a-c-e," but the Newspeakers have changed the meaning.

Acts 15 records an instance of the contamination by Newspeak. Those from Oceania are attempting to change grace into a mixture, a combination of "believe in Jesus and keep the Law." Their thinking was, "We have all these gentiles coming into the church; we must control them, and the control is the Law of Moses. We'll accept them if they'll believe in Jesus and keep the Law for salvation and we'll like them if they keep the Law in order to be spiritual." In Newspeak, "grace" means "works."

Paul had earlier returned from his first missionary trip and had established churches in the ancient world; gentiles had responded to the gospel of grace, God's offer of salvation without strings. God had saved them by grace, justified them by grace and was teaching them by grace. To put the Mosaic Law into salfivic play, to bring in the Law as something necessary for salvation and for present tense sanctification for the spiritual man, would bring the collapse of these new churches. Paul had preached no such thing. Such a new definition of grace would blast Paul's work to powder. The churches would be in pieces across the world. The carrying out of the Great Commission would be over.

God used Paul, Peter, Barnabas, and James to save the day for grace. The Law wasn't to be a requirement for salvation because it was a "yoke" on the necks of the Jews who found it impossible to keep after a thousand years of trying to bear it.

Acts 15 contains the minutes of that meeting, a meeting in which the men from Oceania were sent packing. But the problem is that few today have read and understood the minutes of that historic meeting. The Holy Spirit-directed conclusion was that the Mosaic Law was never a means of salvation and, as of the cross, God abolished that which was written and engraved in stone as a rule of life (II Corinthians 3; Hebrews 7).

NEWSPEAK LIVES

The Newspeakers from Jerusalem lived on to fight another day. Acts 15 should have been a stake in the belly of the legalistic beast, but that was not to be. The hubris of humanity demands the human being have an active part to play in salvation. Pride doesn't tolerate a salvational stage with no human role to play.

When we read the book of Galatians, Paul's fiery polemic for grace, we see that after Paul left the area, certain men introduced the lexicon of Newspeak to the new believers, teaching them that grace is works, so that, they said, to gain eternal life, one must perform the Law and all believers are to put on its yoke.

We might think that after Paul had read the false teachers the riot act, all would have been well. But hubris dies a long and lingering death; it drinks the elixir of human pride to rejuvenate itself over the ages. Like vampires, the legalists drink from the bloody Law and gain renewed energy.

THE PETRI DISH

Newspeak lived on after the Apostles; "Grace is works." Newspeak didn't breathe its last as of the Galatian epistle, but found a theological petri dish in which to breed its infection in the writings of the Church Fathers.

"Let us clothe ourselves with concord and humility, ever exercising self-control, standing far off from all whispering and evil-speaking, *being justified by our works, and not our words.*" Later, the same author writes, "*On account of his hospitality and godliness, Lot was saved out of Sodom.*" Those words, employing Newspeak, changed grace into works, holding that Lot's justification came from his godliness (one might argue against his godliness) and hospitality (argumentation could also continue on this point). The works, not the words, justify, according to Clement of Rome, vaunted Church Father, writing around 96 AD.

Newspeak continued in the writings of Polycarp, a pupil of John, who weighs in on salvation by grace:

> Now He that raised Him from the dead will raise us also; if we (1) do His will and (2) walk in His commandments and (3) love the things which He loved, (4) abstaining from all unrighteousness, (5) covetousness, (6) love of money, (7) evil speaking, (8) false witness; (9) not rendering evil for evil or (10) railing for railing or (11) blow for blow or (12) cursing for cursing . . . [Numerals added]

With this enumeration of twelve things to do, grace is gone. Salvation, conditioned on "if," has twelve strings. Salvation involves the two categories of "abstaining from" and "not rendering." There is no difference between

Polycarp and the Pharisees who were building their own portfolio righteousness. Polycarp's list shows the inherent, logical impossibility of salvation embedded in the strings. Is there anyone in all of church history who has "abstained from *all* unrighteousness?" We would wonder if Polycarp read with understanding what his teacher wrote in I John 1:8-10, "If we claim to be without sin, we deceive ourselves and the truth is not in us. If we confess our sins, he is faithful and just and will forgive us our sins and purify us from all unrighteousness. If we claim we have not sinned, we make him out to be a liar and his word has no place in our lives." Polycarp builds salvation on an "if" based on works. If he read I John 1:8-10, he either never understood it or became confused later.

"Thus," He saith, "they that desire to see Me, and to attain unto My kingdom, must lay hold on Me *through tribulation and affliction.*" So wrote Barnabas, a Church Father who lived from 100-150 AD, one who held that salvation comes via suffering for Christ's sake. Salvation through *our* suffering? What happened to *Christ's* suffering? It's gone. We're now on center stage, suffering our way to earn our ticket into the kingdom.

HOW DID THEY MISS IT?

What happened? What was in the minds of these Church Fathers? Their misunderstanding came because, although they read the word "grace," they didn't understand that word with its Bible definition. The content they put into "grace" was not a biblical one. The Bible word, "grace," comes with the Bible's definition: God's direct intervention of unmerited favor to man. But they didn't read it with that meaning.

Torrance writes in *The Doctrine of Grace in the Apostolic Fathers* that there were contributing factors which led to the misunderstanding of grace:

1. The letters of Paul were not much in general circulation before about 110 AD. Thus, the Mosaic Law still had a powerful influence on the Fathers who emphasized a striving after righteousness, with grace only coming in ad hoc. Grace was put into the framework, "By your works you will be judged."

2. The minds of the Fathers were Greek ones. In the usage of the second century, grace had to do with attractiveness and with a reward for a favor, much like our word, "gratuity," a tip given for good service after we eat. Taken in that sense, one had to strive for grace, one had to become worthy of it. This would negate the Bible's definition completely. When the nuance of "attractiveness" was employed, "the grace of our Lord Jesus Christ" was understood to mean "the attractiveness of our Lord Jesus Christ." This nuance to grace still holds the minds of some who see a talented figure skater and pronounce her as full of grace in form and movement.

Since "words are the dress of thought," grace came dressed as works to the Apostolic Fathers.

People ask, "How could they have missed it; so close to the Apostles' generation?" But remember that there was false doctrine all over the place even during the time of the Apostles and in the churches founded by the Apostles. Paul writes Galatians because the believers there had been "so soon removed," "so soon bewitched" by false teaching. The Corinthians were in danger of being seduced by the pagan philosophy of no resurrection from the dead. The Holy Spirit directs Jude to write to "defend the faith, once and for all delivered to the saints." Then we read of two believers who "have shipwrecked their faith. Among them are Hymenaeus and Alexander, whom I [Paul] have handed over to Satan to be taught not to blaspheme" (I Timothy 1:19-20).

Being with or in the generation immediately after the Apostles is no guarantee that the contemporaneous or near contemporaneous listener gets it. The Church Fathers did not get it and were writers tossed about on every wind of false doctrine that came along. And in so doing, they launched the church on choppy waters for over a thousand years.

TODAY'S SIREN SONG

There continue to be calls to return to the Fathers. In *Church History Through the Ages*, Cairns writes, "The diligent reader of the literature [of the Church Fathers] . . . will find much reward in the way of knowledge and inspiration. It seems somewhat a pity that these writings of edification should have been neglected by the church throughout the ages" (p. 79).

Theologian David Warner, interviewed on March 29, 2007, said:

> The Fathers can inform and challenge Christians of every description. Protestants can rediscover their forgotten roots. This in turn often results in an increased appreciation for Catholic, Eastern Orthodox, and other Episcopal and liturgical traditions.
>
> In other cases, openness to the Fathers becomes a steppingstone toward embracing what we believe to be the fullness of Christian faith and practice found within the Catholic Church.

Catholics can and should rediscover some of the patristic priorities that modern evangelicals are noted for, including: living in and for Christ; reverencing and studying the Bible as the unique, authoritative written word of God; and becoming better informed and enthusiastic witnesses to Jesus Christ, the one and only savior of the world.

We can reaffirm our Catholic tradition of promoting all of the gifts of the Spirit—including the charismatic and hierarchical gifts—toward the end of Christian maturity and unity. All of these distinctive traits are clearly taught and modeled in the Fathers.

One would wonder how a person, reading the Fathers, can become a "better informed and enthusiastic witness to Jesus Christ, the one and only savior of the world," when they learn a false gospel from the Fathers—one with no assurance, filled with works.

Why follow the Church Fathers? Robert Webber gives his affirmation to such a return by writing that the church needs to "recover the universally accepted framework of faith that originated with the apostles, was developed by the Fathers, and has been handed down by the church in its liturgical and theological traditions."

A return to the Church Fathers? Why go back to those who most certainly did not develop the "framework of faith that originated with the apostles," why go back to those who took the nail of grace out of the framework, the one thing which held it together? Why return to those various ones who at various times taught that God would save everyone and that Mary was a perpetual virgin (Origen); that the bread and wine became the body and blood of Jesus when consecrated (Chrysostom);

that salvation came through baptism (Athanasius); that there is a Purgatory, that infants should be baptized, that there are mortal and venial sins, that we should pray to the dead, do penance for sins, get absolution from a priest, that we should recognize Mary as sinless, and give scriptural authority to the Apocrypha (Augustine).

When we turn to that primer for new believers written during the time of the Church Fathers, the Didache, we find this humorous bit of instruction to the convert on the subject of fasting in Chapter 8: "And let not your fastings be with the hypocrites, for they fast on the second and fifth day of the week, but do ye keep your fast on the fourth and on the preparation (the sixth) day." In order not to be hypocritical, the believer has only to fast on different days than the hypocrites? Are we to return to this?

Why should we return to the Fathers? As Loraine Boettner points out: ". . . the body of tradition is not of divine origin nor apostolic [as] is proved by the fact that some traditions contradict others. The church fathers repeatedly contradict one another. When a Roman Catholic priest is ordained he solemnly vows to interpret the Scriptures only 'according to the unanimous consent of the fathers.' But such unanimous consent is purely a myth. The fact is they scarcely agree on any doctrine. They contradict each other, and even themselves as they change their minds and affirm what they previously had denied. . . . the early church fathers condemned the use of images in worship, while later ones approved such use. . . . The early fathers almost unanimously advocated the reading and free use of the Scriptures, while the later ones restricted such reading and use" (*Roman Catholicism*, pp. 78-79).

LUTHER AGAINST THE FATHERS

It was not an overnight event, but Luther came to realize that the doctrinal underpinnings of the church he loved and had given his life to serve were founded on tradition, not the Bible. It is because of that realization that Luther has left for us one of the great statements of church history. At the Diet of Worms in 1521, Luther was called to the court of Holy Roman Emperor Charles V by ecclesiastical prosecutors to recant of his writings or die.

There were the threats of excommunication. Charles V demanded a complete recantation from Luther concerning the books he had written. They charged that he was divisive since many who read his books were questioning the Roman Church and the system of popery. But Luther was calling everyone back to the authority of Scripture and away from the traditions of the fathers.

Under examination, he agreed that the books were his, but he asked for time to pray before answering the charges against him. He asked for time to further consider his answers. Request granted. The next day he was called back to court. The prosecutor demanded to know if Luther would recant or not. In a statement that has cemented itself in our mystic cords of memory for over five hundred years, Luther said:

Unless I am convinced by the testimony of the Holy Scriptures or by evident reason—for I can believe neither pope nor councils alone, as it is clear that they have erred repeatedly and contradicted themselves—I consider myself convicted by the testimony of Holy Scripture, which is my basis; *my conscience is captive to the Word of God.* Thus I cannot and will not recant, because acting against one's conscience is neither safe nor sound. God help me. Amen.

Luther asked, "What good does it do to rely on the venerable old Fathers who have been approved over such a long succession of ages? Were they too not all equally blind or rather, did they not simply overlook the clearest and most explicit statements of Paul?"

To issue a call to return to contradictory traditions in which one author writes one thing and then later the opposite, to issue a call to return the authors who also write in contradiction to the others is to return to the illogic of folly.

In Newspeak, "Grace is works," and the confusion continues. The influence of the Church Fathers is immense. Newspeak is embedded in Roman Catholic theology: "We Catholics insist that James 2:14–26 shows that works are more than mere evidence of faith. Works actually justify." (Kenneth J. Howell, *Catholic Answers* website).

TODAY'S NEWSPEAK NONSENSE

A Protestant turned Catholic writes, "Works are necessary for salvation, and, in fact, are one of the principle determining factors in whether or not one obtains salvation. We say this with the proviso that Paul outrightly [sic] condemns works done with a view toward *obligating* God to pay the worker with salvation. Man can never put God in the position of being in debt to an imperfect and sinful creature. The only way God can accept our works is through his grace. Works done under the auspices of God's grace, that is, works done that do not demand payment from God but are rewarded only due to the kindness and mercy of God, are the works that Paul requires for salvation" (Robert A. Sungenis, *Not by Faith Alone: The Biblical Evidence for the Catholic Doctrine of Justification*, p. 46 [italics his]).

This is Newspeak nonsense. Newspeak puts words in Paul's quill, words he never wrote. Paul never wrote that there are two types of works, works which try to obligate God and works which do not demand a payment from God. Paul saw *all* his works in his pre-conversion days and counted "them" (not "part of them") as "rubbish" in Philippians 3. When Paul was the worker-man for salvation, Saul, he believed he was doing God's will with his works, even the "good" work of persecuting the Church, which he said he did in ignorance. Later, he came to agree with Isaiah, "All our righteousnesses are as filthy rags." Not some of them, but all of them are such filth that they don't count.

Paul writes in Romans 4:4-5: "Now when a man works, his wages are not credited to him as a gift, but as an obligation. However, to the man who does not work but trusts God who justifies the wicked, his faith is credited as righteousness." Paul doesn't see two types of works, works which obligate God and works which don't; he bluntly says, "Works obligate."

Newspeak destroys assurance of salvation—who can discern his motivation—"Am I doing this to earn salvation or am I doing this without obligating God in any way?"

As Paul revealed, it is either Christ's righteousness or our righteousness, not a blended percentage of both. Our righteousness doesn't make the grade. There is no partnership in salvation in which I do my part (supply good works "without obligating God") and He does His part (supply whatever percentage is needed to make up the lack of works which do not obligate Him).

Jesus said, "No one comes to the Father except through Me." This sentence completely excludes any type of good works, even the ones not obligating God, which is an artificial distinction read into Paul and the rest of the New Testament. To Paul, works are works, and all are salvific slime.

Using Newspeak as the language of choice without realizing it, a writer posted this statement: "Works are not required for salvation, but they are necessary." That's Newspeak at its nonsensical best, as is the statement, "We are saved by faith alone, but the faith which saves is never alone." Newspeak is clearly seen by the fact that, by its very definition, the faith which saves is never alone, so how can faith alone save? Logicians would have a field day with that nonsense. It's as if someone said, "A slender obese man who was tall and short climbed eight flights of stairs to get to the basement." It is as if someone read this sentence in a college catalog, "Algebra I is a prerequisite for Algebra II, but Algebra I is not required for enrollment in Algebra II."

Newspeak has bewitched us for a long time. Paul, Peter, Barnabas, and James fought it in Acts 15. Paul, stunned by the fact that the Galatians were defecting from grace, the Bible word with the Bible's definition, produced a polemic called Galatians against their desertion.

Newspeak continues to hypnotize, paralyzing logic and rational thought, mesmerizing people to believe statements at one and the same time irrational, illogical, internally contradictory, and therefore deadly.

NEWSPEAK HIDES IN HYMNS AND SONGS

The melodies beguile us into singing Newspeak. Newspeak loves to sing: "All to Jesus I Surrender," a hymn which includes the words, "All to Jesus I surrender. . . take me Jesus, take me now." And, "All to Jesus I surrender; now I feel the sacred flame. Oh, the joy of full salvation! Glory to His name!" It appears that the hymn is teaching that if one surrenders all and then asks for divine acceptance, then Jesus will "take" him. In the last verse, the song concludes with, "full salvation" only coming at the surrendering.

Newspeak can be obvious or hidden in the familiar, even in the simplest of songs. We have taught millions of children to sing Newspeak: "Jesus loves me, this I know, for the Bible tells me so. . . . If I love Him when I die, He will take me to His home on high." *If*? There is no *if* in grace; there are no conditions.

TRADITION

"Grace" has an ancient tradition in Newspeak, a tradition which continues to confuse and lead astray. But what is tradition? G. K. Chesterton wrote: "Tradition means giving a vote to most obscure of all classes, our ancestors. It is the democracy of the dead." Liberating grace from the votes of the democracy of the dead means giving that amazing Bible word its amazing Bible definition. Without that definition, grace is not amazing.

CHAPTER TWO

NEWSPEAK: "FINISHED IS INCOMPLETE"

"And on the seventh day, God rested." This rest was not the surcease because of exhaustion; it was the rest that comes when there is nothing left to do. God had finished what He had begun. The work of making a home for the king of the earth, man, was over and done. God had provided everything necessary for him to live and move and have his being on this planet. Earth, the only planet created for man in the universe, is one of a kind. Other planets may be bigger, but none better.

Only this planet has air man can breathe; only this planet has water man can drink; only this planet has food man can eat. Outside the earth, the universe is a killer, hostile to man. The human being can breathe in no other place but here. If he leaves the earth, he must take his oxygen, food, and water with him because he hasn't found those bare necessities anywhere else. Looking through telescopes and examining through probes, he has found no air he can breathe, no food he can eat, no water he can drink other than here on earth, the prepared planet.

When God finished His creative work, all He had done was good. There was not one thing more to be done to sustain the life of the unique creation, the human being.

FAMOUS LAST WORDS

Thousands of years after finishing creation's work, the God-Man, hands and feet rendered immobile by nails made of the metal He created, gasping for one more breath of the oxygen He created, shouted something. We might expect someone dying the cruelest death the creatures He had made could invent to shout what many a dying criminal had shouted as they hung on crosses— curses spat at those who had nailed them there.

No curses. Instead they heard, "Father, forgive them for they know not what they do." They heard a question, "My God, My God, why have you forsaken Me?" Then they could listen to the tender words, "Mother behold your son; son, behold your mother."

Then they heard this climactic exclamation point: "It is finished!"

NO NEED TO STAND

Thirty years later, the author of Hebrews is writing about the goings on in the Temple, a structure which had only a few years left to stand before the Romans would come, leveling it to the ground. He writes about the activities in the Temple, pointing out how the priests everyday offered the lambs, the bulls, and the goats to God, one blood-letting after another inside that building. They were doing what thousands of priests before them had done, offering sacrifices for their own sins and the sins of the people.

They never stopped. Over the previous generations, priests came in waves and in shifts. When one died, another took his place. In the performance of all their duties, they found no chair in which to sit. They were on duty, always on duty, always going about their bloody business, a business never ultimately resolved, and a business from which there was no rest and no closure in their lifetimes. Sin in the camp never ceased; they always needed one more bull, one more goat, another lamb, another calf. The Temple's maw for sacrifices was neither closed nor satisfied. The Temple kept crying, "More!"

The God-Man who shouted, "It is finished" was a priest, One from a different order; not of Aaron, but of Melchizedek. After His ascension, He did what no other priest on duty had done; He sat down at the right hand of God the Father and He sat down because His work was so complete that He pronounced it once and for all finished.

The work He finished was the work of paying the penalty for our sins. As the author of Hebrews wrote, "He did it once; He did it once for all."

ENTER NEWSPEAK

The finished work of Christ. The phrase rolls off the churchly tongue so easily; it's a cliché in the halls of the ecclesiastics. And it is with this word that Newspeak has done its work, because in Newspeak, "finished" doesn't mean "finished." "Finished" means "incomplete."

Enter the ancient Newspeakers, the Church Fathers. Listen to them as they write how, at baptism, one's sins are forgiven up to that moment in time. All sins. But that forgiveness doesn't extend to sins committed *after* baptism. Christ's work took care of pre-baptismal sins, but not those committed afterward, they said. At baptism, the new believer enjoyed a clean slate, but post baptismal sins would soon sully the slate, and the dicta of I John 1:8, 10 would roar to the fore.

As far as pre-baptismal sins were concerned, Christ's work was finished. But in regard to those sins after the new believer came out of the water, Christ's finished work was declared incomplete by the Church Fathers.

We saw in the previous chapter that Newspeak never dies. Although some today may not hold that one's Christian life begins at baptism, they still use Newspeak in such a way that finished means incomplete. There are those who tell us that there are some sins, some especially heinous sins which a believer can commit after he becomes a Christian, that Christ's finished work isn't complete when it comes to those really abominable ones.

THE INSERTED BLANKS IN GALATIANS 5

They point to the sin list in Galatians 5 as being so atrocious, the offences on the list knock one out of heaven: "sexual immorality, impurity and debauchery; idolatry and witchcraft; _____, _____, _____, _____, _____, and _____. I warn you, as I did before, that those who live like this will not inherit the kingdom of God."

Did Paul put blanks in the sentence? No. The Newspeak speakers do. Whenever they talk about those sins which will bar entrance into heaven, they list the aforementioned ones; they don't list those in the blanks (Paul did) because they're too common in their own (and every other believers') lives.

"Hatred, discord, jealousy, fits of rage, selfish am-
bition, dissensions, factions and envy" should appear
in those blanks because that's what Paul wrote. In my
experience, in every case, I've yet to hear a declaration
that envy (or discord or jealousy or a fit of rage) will
send the believer to hell. Paul isn't writing about salvation; he's writing about "inheriting." The believer can
lose an *inheritance* of rewards in the kingdom, not his
salvation.

The point is that, in the language of Newspeak, there
are some sins for which Christ didn't die, and therefore,
"finished" in Newspeak becomes "incomplete." To
put Newspeak in the context of Hebrews, Christ our
High Priest can't sit down when it comes to some sins.
He must stand and stand helplessly because what He
declared finished wasn't finished after all.

SUICIDE

One of the most enduring of ideas is that Christ's work
is unfinished concerning suicide, that is, His death can't
cover that one. We have Thomas Aquinas, "The Angelic
Doctor" to thank for that concept. He devoted much
space to the subject of suicide in his massive work, *Summa
Theologica*, where he wrote, "Suicide is the most fatal of
sins because it cannot be repented of" (2-2. q. 64, 5).

The poet Dante, following Aquinas's theology, placed
those who take their own lives on the seventh level of
hell, below the greedy and the murderous (*Inferno* 13).
For centuries those who committed the unconfessed and
therefore unforgivable sin of suicide were not buried in
cemeteries that Catholic priests had consecrated.

Aquinas's dictum hasn't been quarantined to Roman Catholic theology, but is a view widely held by

Protestants today. Though not officially the stated
doctrine of Protestants, one finds that many rank and
file classify suicide as the unpardonable sin, an idea
they've picked up by osmosis—it's something they've
always heard, so, "It's in the Bible somewhere."

Newspeak cuts at the very heart of the work of
Christ, destroying it. It portrays Christ's work as not
good enough, even though Romans 8 says that nothing
in the future ("nothing" includes our sins in the future)
will be able to separate us from the love of God.

"Finished means incomplete" cuts the ground from
under the believer's assurance. If His work wasn't finished, then there are some sins lurking out there which
I could commit and in the commission, lose it all. For
the believer who is confused by Newspeak, his life can
be one worry after another every waking moment.

THE FALL OF THE DOMINOES

"Finished means incomplete" causes other dominoes to
teeter and fall. In I John 2:2 we read, "He is the atoning
sacrifice for our sins, and not only for ours but also for the
sins of the whole world." "Atoning sacrifice" is "propitia-
tion," that is, an "appeasement" or a "satisfaction." Christ
is the "satisfaction" for our sins.

It's inconceivable that God's holiness and justice
could be satisfied with an unfinished sacrifice. Just as
He was satisfied with the finished work of the six days
of creation, so He is satisfied with Christ's atoning sacrifice because it was finished. Since it's finished, there is
nothing we can add to it, for who can add anything to
what has been finished once for all?

But if finished means incomplete, we must add to the
cross-work of Christ by building our own righteousness,

by giving up sins, or at best, trying to. If we have to add to what's unfinished, we must add to His work our deeds, but again we wind up with no sure word; who can know when he's done enough for long enough to complete what Christ didn't finish?

What has the evangelist from Oceania to offer the unbeliever? An incomplete work of Christ. He can only offer the invitation, "Believe in Jesus and receive eternal life, which isn't really eternal because I don't know and you don't know if you're going to keep it by giving up enough sins and by doing enough for long enough, and after all is said and done, you might lose it anyway if you sin big enough." ("Big enough" being interpreted as "any sin the evangelist would never commit.") At best, the evangelist can only offer a temporary eternal life which is Newspeak all over again. If something is "eternal," it cannot be "temporary," or "temporarily eternal."

Once Newspeak changes words, because the doctrinal framework of the Bible is so tightly constructed, other doctrinal dominoes begin to fall because "eternal life" now means "eternal until-you-sin-life." And the eternal security domino has fallen.

In Colossians 2, Paul wrote, "When you were dead in your sins and in the uncircumcision of your sinful nature, God made you alive with Christ. He forgave us *all* our sins . . ." When "finished" means "incomplete," then "all" means "some of." Another domino has fallen. Newspeak all over again. In Newspeak, when "finished" is "incomplete," then forgiveness is for some sins and not for others; the death of Christ is for some sins and not others. In Newspeak, "all" means "some of."

The finished work of Christ means that salvation isn't a partnership in which the sinner does his part (offering 5%, 10%, 20% good deeds) and God does His part (supplying the needed 95%, 90%, or 80%). Salvation is neither a bargaining process nor a deal. Since Christ's work is finished, the sinner makes no contribution to his salvation. If salvation is unfinished, then Christ's incomplete work needs the sinner's help.

FINISHED IN HISTORY

"The finished work of Christ" is the phrase that struck the teenager Hudson Taylor, bringing him to his knees, praising God. Frank Boreham tells the story:

> The day on which James Hudson Taylor—then a boy in his teens—found himself confronted by that tremendous text was, as he himself testified in old age, "a day that he could never forget." It is a day that China can never forget; a day that the world can never forget. It was a holiday; everybody was away from home; and the boy found time hanging heavily upon his hands.
>
> In an aimless way he wandered, during the afternoon, into his father's library, and poked about among the shelves. "I tried," he says, "to find some book with which to while away the leaden hours. Nothing attracting me, I turned over a basket of pamphlets and selected from among them a tract that looked interesting. I knew that it would have a story at the commencement and a moral at the close; but I promised myself that I would enjoy the story and leave the rest. It would be easy to put away the tract as soon as it should seem prosy."
>
> He scampers off to the stable loft, throws himself on the hay, and plunges into the book. He is captivated by the narrative, and finds it impossible to drop the book when the story comes to an end.

He reads on and on. He is rewarded by one great golden word whose significance he has never before discovered: "The Finished Work of Christ!" The theme entrances him; and at last he only rises from his bed in the soft hay that he may kneel on the hard floor of the loft and surrender his young life to the Savior who had surrendered everything for him. If, he asked himself, as he lay upon the hay, if the whole work was finished, and the whole debt paid upon the Cross, what is there left for me to do? "And then," he tells us, "there dawned upon me the joyous conviction that there was nothing in the world to be done but to fall upon my knees, accept the Savior and praise Him for evermore."

"It is finished!" "When Jesus, therefore, had received the vinegar he said, 'It is finished!' and He bowed His head and gave up the ghost."

"Then there dawned upon me the joyous conviction that, since the whole work was finished and the whole debt paid upon the Cross, there was nothing for me to do but to fall upon my knees, accept the Savior and praise Him for evermore!"

Here we see that a teenager can see the salvific implications of "finished." It doesn't take a degree or training in theology to understand that "finished" means "finished."

Three hundred years earlier, the realization of the finished work of Christ brought another to his knees and changed the world:

His sole consolation was studying the Bible; it was then that he felt closest to God. One day, he meditated on the truth of Romans 1:17: "For in it [the gospel] the righteousness of God is revealed from faith to faith; as it is written, 'But the righteous man shall live by faith.'"

This was the answer. Luther wept as he accepted Christ's finished work on the cross as full payment for his sin. He was free at last, and new joy filled his heart. When he began preaching and teaching at the University of Wittenberg, people flocked to hear his vibrant messages. (Bainton)

This is a reversal of what we saw in the previous chapter in which man did his part (X number of good works) and God did His part to take up the slack (Y amount of grace). This is a reversal in the sense that, if His work is unfinished, He has done His part, but the sinner must supply what His work left incomplete. Do not such statements border on or cross the line into blasphemy?

Dr. Charles Ryrie points out in the Ryrie Study Bible that we have found the word, "finished" written across tax bills in the ancient world and the word was good news to the taxpayer: "Paid in full." We might ask, "What part of 'in full' is not clear?"

Spurgeon, with his usual but amazing rhetorical flourish, leaves no doubt about the completeness of Christ's work:

Now, concerning this ransom, we have to observe, that it was *all paid,* and all paid *at once.* When Christ redeemed his people, he did it thoroughly; he did not leave a single debt unpaid, nor yet one farthing for them to settle afterwards. God demanded of Christ the payment for the sins of all his people; Christ stood forward, and to the utmost farthing paid whate'er his people owed.

The sacrifice of Calvary was not a part payment; it was not a partial exoneration, it was a complete and perfect payment, and it obtained a complete and perfect remittal of all the debts of all believers that have lived, do live, or shall live, to the very end of time. On that day when Christ hung on the cross, he did not leave a single farthing for us to pay as a satisfaction to God; he did not leave, from a thread even to a shoe-latchet, that he had not satisfied. The whole of the demands of the law were paid down there and then by Jehovah Jesus, the great high priest of all his people. And blessed be his name, he paid it all at once too. So priceless was the ransom, so princely and munificent was the price demanded for our souls, one might have thought it would have been marvelous if Christ had paid it by installments; some of it now, and some of it then. King's ransoms have sometimes been paid part at once, and part in dues afterwards, to run through years.

But not so our Savior: once for all he gave himself a sacrifice; at once he counted down the price, and said, "It is finished," leaving nothing for him to do, nor for us to accomplish. He did not drivel out a part-payment, and then declare that he would come again to die, or that he would again suffer, or that he would again obey; but down upon the nail, to the utmost farthing, the ransom of all people was paid, and a full receipt given to them, and Christ nailed that receipt to his cross, and said, "It is done, it is done; I have taken away the handwriting of ordinances, I have nailed it to the cross; who is he that shall condemn my people, or lay anything to their charge? for I have blotted out like a cloud their transgressions, and like a thick cloud their sins!"

When, by the illuminating work of the Holy Spirit, a person understands the impact of "finished," the salvific light dawns. When the clutter and confusion of Newspeak is removed, the sinner sees that Christ's work is enough for the person to become saved forever. As one person wrote, "For though I had believed that Christ's death was necessary to go to heaven, I finally understood that Christ's finished work was enough to be saved forever. . . . My sins had been paid in full by Jesus Christ at Calvary and there was nothing left for me to do but simply put my faith in the crucified and risen savior, the Lord Jesus Christ." (Dennis Rokser, quoted in *The Gospel of the Christ*, p. 14)

When the sinner realizes the full weight of "finished," without the cluttering and confusing influence of Newspeak, he realizes that saving faith occurs when the right content is believed about the right object of the faith. It is then that he sees that to have faith in one's works plus faith in Jesus is not saving faith because by placing his faith in his works *and* Jesus, "finished" becomes "incomplete" and he is not placing his faith in Christ alone, but in Christ plus himself.

EITHER THE GOSPEL OR A FALSE ONE

Words are important and there are no more important words to the human race than the words of the Bible. Those words are there to communicate truth; the concepts those words communicate are not there to be tampered with and changed, thus changing the truth into something else. Either "finished" means "finished" or if, because of Newspeak, it means something else. If it means something else other than finished, it's part of "another gospel," one which does not save (Galatians 1:6-9).

From the parched throat of the God-Man on the cross, we hear, "I thirst." A soldier callously offers

Him a sponge soaked with the cheap sour wine used to constrict the throat and throttle the screams of the crucified. Yet, Jesus, the giver of living water, manages the triumphant shout of grace which the human race has needed to hear since Genesis 3:15: "It is finished!"

CHAPTER THREE

NEWSPEAK: "REPENTANCE IS PENANCE"

The English language is rich. According to *Ask Oxford*, English is a linguistic treasure chest containing over a quarter of a million words, although the Oxford Answer Men admit that knowing the number of words in a language is impossible.

We English speakers have inherited a language which carries with it a huge vocabulary. The vocabularies of living languages such as English are always changing. It's part of linguistic life. "Cool" no longer refers only to temperature; "hot" has evolved to mean "good-looking."

WORDS EVOLVE

It's a compliment to hear that you're a "nice person," but it was not always so. Five hundred years ago in the linguistic evolutionary process, if someone said you were "nice," those were fighting words, mister. That's because "nice" originally meant "stupid." "Nice" had quite an evolutionary path. By the 16th century, if you were "nice," you were "very particular" or "finicky." Three hundred years later, in the 19th century, a "nice person was "pleasant or agreeable" and then "respectable." This progression shows how a word can come to have a completely different meaning from its beginnings. Rob Kyff, a teacher and writer in West Hartford, writes on how words change their meanings:

> The first time I went to a restaurant as a boy (a rare and exciting treat in those days), I noticed that the menu described the main courses as "entrees."
>
> Associating this word with "entries," I immediately pictured the food selections as horses lined up at the starting gate, ready to compete. It's Spaghetti in the lead by a noodle, with Steak sizzling in second and Chicken bringing up the rear!
>
> In fact, my instinct wasn't far off. "Entrée" is, in fact, derived from the Old French "entree," which meant "to enter." And we still use "entree" to mean "permission or right to entry" when we say, "My friendship with the owner provided an entree into the company."
>
> During the 1700s, "entrée" also developed a specific culinary meaning. Back then, formal dining brought forth an endless succession of courses—soup, salad, fish, berries, shrubs, meat, old shoes, nuts (hence, our expression "soup to nuts").
>
> The centerpiece of such a meal was invariably the roast. So, the light course or appetizer served just before the roast was dubbed the "entree" because it served as a kind of entrance to the main course.
>
> When dining became less elaborate and fewer courses were offered, the term 'entrée' somehow came to denote the main course. Perhaps this was by mistake, or perhaps it reflected our fondness for using pretentious French words to describe foods, even if the meaning of those words is ambiguous.

Words aren't married to their definitions 'til death do them part. The word "repent" is one of those words which Newspeak has divorced from its original meaning, and like all divorces, caused confusion and havoc. In a movie about the trials and tribulations of divorce, one of the divorced men laments, "It's never over!" The confusion surrounding "repent" is never over.

Because of the divorce and "repent" being given a meaning it never had, "repent" as "feel sorry for" is like a computer chip embedded in people's minds, so that when they hear "repent," they can't help but think, "feel sorry for sin."

VISION, VISION, WHO'S GOT A VISION?

This phenomenon is akin to what we read in Proverbs 29:18: "Where there is no vision, the people perish." Every month the pastor of a church will receive at least one piece of mass mail-out inviting him to attend a church growth seminar in which the expansion of the church will be guaranteed if he will come to the seminar and hear various lectures on various topics and one of those topics is surely to be "Leading the Way to Growth: Casting a Vision for Your Church."

After they read enough of this literature, well-meaning pastors will often say, "I am a visionary leader. I will cast a vision, a goal, and everyone is to unite in with this goal." Then you hear them quote, "Without a vision . . ." (But note the ellipsis; he always leaves out the last part of the verse, which gives the context.)

What's going on here? One man assumes that he has heard from God for a group of people. He shares his dreams, his desires with that church and if they like it, they hire him. They have a vision, his vision.

Although there's no command in the New Testament that the leader(s) of the church write a vision statement, the church growth literature will often cite Proverbs 29:18 as some sort of the Pastor's Great Commission. So often have pastors read and heard this verse, as explained in the church growth literature, so often have they heard it in the seminars, that the word has been embedded in their minds as meaning, "You determine your vision of the hope and future for your church, then collect followers to climb the mountain with you." They say this vision will unite your church because, now they know where they're going, where you're leading them, and what their hopes and dreams are to be for a glorious future.

But the problem is that the implant is incorrect. Even without knowing the Hebrew or the context, the pastor should know something is wrong in that Christ is the Leader of the church. Christ is the vision of the church; His Great Commission is the purpose of the church, so the pastor doesn't need to write his own. Proverbs 29:18 is not telling the pastor to pray for a vision for his church (and who said it was "his" church in the first place?).

Although the leaders in the church growth movement shun preaching from the King James Version, it's interesting that's the version to which they go for the translation of this verse. Had they known Hebrew or had they read the rest of the verse (which they don't quote) they would see from the context (Context is king!) their explanation of the sentence is wrong, wrong, wrong. Had they even read the New King James Version, they would see the mistake of the vision-casting church growth movement.

Proverbs 29:18, literally translated, says: "Where there is no revelation, the people cast off restraint" (NKJV); "Where there is no revelation, the people cast off restraint" (NIV).

The author isn't writing about a pastor's personal vision for a church; he's writing about divine revelation, i.e., the Bible. In this specific case, the Mosaic Law is the revelation. Where there are no absolutes, when people cast off the absolutes of God's Word, it kills them, they die, literally,

LUTHER ON 16TH AVENUE

In the 1500s humanism was carrying the day, and contrary to the opinion of many, that was a good thing in regard to the Bible. Biblical humanism was a return to the Greek and Hebrew manuscripts of the Old and New Testaments. Rather than going by the Latin of Jerome, biblical humanists returned to the Greek of Paul, Peter, Matthew, and Mark. The New Testament became a book in living color.

Biblical humanism with its emphasis on the original languages of Scripture made a tremendous impact when Luther began to read the New Testament in the Koine Greek, the language of the New Testament.

The song, "16th Avenue," is about aspiring songwriters in Nashville, Tennessee. They meet together to play and sing their compositions, each one hoping for a hit. As the song tells the story, one night it happened and a hit was born: "But then one night in some empty room, where no curtains ever hung, like a miracle, some golden words rolled off someone's tongue . . ."

One day as Luther was studying the Greek New Testament in an empty room, he made a startling discovery: Jerome's translation of repent as "do penance" was Newspeak. He knew that the literal meaning was "a change of mind," and by this discovery, the bulwark of the Roman system, penance, came crashing down. From that moment on, Luther began to "storm the Pope." Bible words with Bible definitions have their consequences.

THE BLOATING OF REPENTANCE

In Oceania, repentance involves much more than changing one's mind; in Newspeak the word has to do with works and feelings such as contrition, confession, and the performance of acts of penance. The penitent must feel a certain

way ("sorry for his sins"), he must admit his sins, and after
that, he becomes his own atonement through penance. What
is this other than Oceania's importation of works into grace?

Continuing in the tradition of Newspeak, Chick Tracts,
wanting to present the gospel in a series of cartoon drawings
show a worried man saying, "Of course I believe the Bible—
and I'm convinced that I'm lost and going to hell—but what
must I do to be saved?"

The man phrases his question in the wording of the
Philippian jailer in Acts 16. The words are identical. When
the guard asked Paul that question, Paul responded, "Believe
on the Lord Jesus Christ and you will be saved."

When a visitor walks into the foyer of many a church,
the concerned and evangelistically minded parishioners
have strategically placed a tract rack to confront the new-
comer. Unfortunately, if he takes a few of these explanatory
brochures and reads them with discernment, he's confused.
He'll read that it's necessary to "believe, repent, surrender,
confess, deny self, yield, forsake all, ask Jesus into his heart,
receive, and accept," depending on which of the tracts
he reads. Even to the casual reader, these tracts aren't in
agreement and conflict with each other. The terms don't
mean the same thing; if they do, then meaningful language
and communication collapse. Some tracts present the above
as steps to salvation and the number of steps varies with
the tract. But in most tracts, there is a not-so-subtle addition
of works to faith and with that addition, grace changes to
works.

The ever-popular Chick Tract in which the worried man
asks, "What must I do to be saved," answers his question:
"REPENT!—Surrender your life to Christ. Acknowledge that
He died for your sins and receive Him as Savior." Repentance
has become penance, the penance of "surrender your life to
Christ."

Paul's answer uses six words; the cartoon panels use eighteen, three times as many. The question is the same; the answers differ. Harry Ironside said, "When anyone comes promising salvation to those 'who make full surrender' of all that they have to God, and who 'pay the price of full salvation' he is preaching another gospel, for the price was paid on Calvary's cross and the work that saves is finished. It was Christ Jesus who made the full surrender when He yielded His life on Calvary that saves us, not our surrender in any way to Him."

Benny Hinn agrees with the Chick tract. He instructs the unbeliever to pray a prayer: "Dear Lord Jesus, I believe You are the Son of God. I believe You came to earth 2,000 years ago. I believe you died for me on the cross and shed Your blood for my salvation. I believe you rose from the dead and ascended on high. I believe You are coming back again to earth. Dear Jesus, I am a sinner. Forgive my sin. Cleanse me now with Your precious blood. Come into my heart. Save my soul right now. I give you my life. I receive You now as my Savior, my Lord, and my God. I am Yours forever, and I will serve You and follow You the rest of my days. From this moment on, I belong to You only. I no longer belong to this world, nor to the enemy of my soul. I belong to You, and I am born again."

With the additions of "I will serve you and follow you for the rest of my days," works has made its successful assault.

The Fellowship Tract League, also using the cartoon format, shows two boys, hands folded in prayer. One of them, speaks: "I prayed to God and told Him I was sorry for my sins; like being a bully and stealing. I promised I wouldn't do those things any more! And He saved me and forgave me of all my sins. I'm going to live in heaven someday!" There is no mention of "believe." According to the information, salvation comes from being sorry and promising not to be a bully and not to steal.

STOP IT!

We see a common idea about repentance, one straight from Newspeak with this definition: "Repent means to stop sinning, whether by acts you commit (sins of commission') or acts you fail to do (sins of omission). Biblical repentance is not merely the cessation of the act, but agreeing with God in your heart, mind, and will that the act was sinful—and that as your motivation to stop sinning. For anyone could stop doing the wrong thing and still embrace it in their hearts. Biblical repentance has as much to do with your agreement with God about your sin as it does the modification of your behavior." The assault on grace is evident in that definition.

Repentance becomes behavior modification to the point of "stop sinning" and "stop wanting to, stop embracing it in your hearts." The writer of that definition seems blind to the fact that even he hasn't stopped sinning. Have any of us stopped sinning and stopped wanting to (I Jn. 1:8, 10)?

To understand how biblical repentance works in a real case scenario, we would understand that those recognizing repentance as a change of mind would tell the adulterer that adultery is sin and that he, a sinner, needs salvation. They would tell him to trust Jesus alone as his Savior who died for all his sins and rose from the dead. By placing his trust in Jesus alone, he would learn that he would be delivered from an eternal hell. Only after salvation is his adultery an issue. It is a matter of discipleship.

However, those from Oceania would tell the adulterer that he must feel sorry for his adultery, confess his adultery, and, along with all other sins, give them up, and stop wanting to commit the act. Then and only then, may he come to Christ.

[There is disagreement among Oceanians over the proper Newspeak definition of repentance in that there are some who would tell him that, after being contrite and after his confession, he must be willing to give up the sin. To some Newspeakers, being willing counts.]

STAMPED IN OUR DNA

In a seminary class at Free Grace Seminary, each student surveyed five people concerning the word "repent." Without exception, the responses were identical—repentance meant the sinner was to feel sorry for his sins and turn from them. In many cases that was the exact wording, showing just how well Jerome has chiseled Newspeak is into the modern mind. In *The Message*, a New Testament paraphrase, Matthew 4:17, reads, "Change your life" for "repent."

This has brought confusion into the gospel as people are told that they must feel a certain way to be saved, turn from their sins to be saved, and change their lives to be saved. Newspeak has an impact on child evangelism because many children would have to work up a feeling of sorrow over sin or else fear they were not saved. I know because I tried. I heard many an evangelist admonish us at revival meetings to feel sorrow for our sins and come forward to "Just as I Am." I wanted the feeling and tried to work it up, just as others tried to do. However, no one ever asked the evangelist, "What if I can't work up the feeling?"

Evangelists exhort people to "come forward and shed tears of repentance." But this leads to confusion among people who don't cry easily. Such invitations present a God who will not save until you say, "I'm sorry." They present a God who has to be coaxed into granting salvation if the tears and remorse were great enough for long enough; and once that idea takes root in the penitent's mind, assurance of salvation is gone because he has no way of knowing if he was contrite enough for long enough. The nagging question comes, "Did I feel sorry enough, deeply enough for long enough?"

WHAT ABOUT II CORINTHIANS 7:8-10?

To defend the idea that repentance means a feeling of sorrow, some point to II Corinthians 7:8-10 where Paul writes, "For even if I made you sad by my letter, I do not regret having written it (even though I did regret it, for I see that my letter made you sad, though only for a short time). Now I rejoice, not because you were made sad, but because you were made sad to the point of repentance. For you were made sad as God intended, so that you were not harmed in any way by us. For sadness as intended by God produces a repentance that leads to salvation, leaving no regret, but worldly sadness brings about death."

Paul is writing in II Corinthians about a letter he wrote to them sometime between First and Second Corinthians. In the letter, Paul was harsh with them and, although he said that he regretted being so hard on them, God had used his epistle to accomplish what was needed — repentance.

As some have read II Corinthians 7, they've pointed to these sentences as proof positive that repent means "feel sorry for." However, after reading the verses, is that what Paul is saying?

One author writes this about II Corinthians 7:8-10: "Repentance means a 'change of mind' and that is exactly what we see in faith (belief)."

So far, so good. But the writer can't restrain himself and continues: "But it [repentance] moves to the heart and repentance is also sorrow. II Corinthians 7:10 says, 'Godly (God given) sorrow brings repentance that leads to salvation, but the sorrow of the world brings death.' The world's sorrow brings regret, feeling bad about what we do, but not being willing to change. Judas 'regretted what he did and went to the priests and said, I am guilty, I have betrayed innocent blood.'" The author doesn't realize the contradiction into which he's written himself. According to his definition, repentance consists of faith plus sorrow which leads to change.

JUDAS HAD THREE THINGS GOING FOR HIM

The betrayer had all three: Judas had faith in the fact that Jesus was innocent; Judas was sorry for what he had done; Judas changed his behavior by returning the money. But believing that Jesus was innocent doesn't save, just as millions of people today believe that Jesus was a good man and teacher. Feeling sorry for sin, just as people feel sorry for what they've done, doesn't save and they make moral reformations of life and practice. None of those things save them just as none of those saved "the son of perdition."

Even a casual reader can see that II Corinthians 7:10 is not a proof text for "repentance = penance" because the "godly sorrow" is not the repentance, but godly sorrow produces the repentance, the change of mind. In the paragraph, "sorrow" and "repentance" are separate. The one (sorrow) produces the other (a change of mind) but is not the change of mind itself.

All sorts of works are imported when Newspeak smuggles "change your life" into "repent." The changes would have to entail a certain number of good works and we're right back to the early fourth century reading from the Vulgate and its making Newspeak ecclesiastically official.

PROTESTANTS AND ROME UNITED

Those reading penance into repentance are reading into the word the same thing Roman Catholicism reads, not realizing it, but in fact, making salvation dependant on human activity. When Protestants do this, the result is the same, although not as "official" as the Roman system with its need for confession on the part of the sinner to a priest, the pardon granted by the priest, and the assignment of the doing of something good to make the absolution active in his experience. Although the route isn't the same for Protestants, the destination is the same, the doing of something good ("change your life") to make up for something bad in order to receive forgiveness.

Newspeak implies that to be saved, a person needs to get good or get better, then come to Christ. By feeling sorry for his sins, by tuning from his sins, and thereby changing his life, he processes himself to the point of coming to Christ. In a sense, he is part of his own atonement.

Such a "gospel" leads to unanswerable questions: "Which sins should I turn from? Selected ones or all of them? For how long should I turn from them? What if I can't turn from all of them? What if I revert back? Assurance becomes impossible.

Paul tells us that salvation is not of works, lest any man should boast. There will be no braggarts in heaven saying, "I'm sure glad I felt sorry for my sins," or "Let me tell you how I changed my life so I could be here." No one will be able to say, "I want to tell you how I gave up smoking to get here."

GOD'S ASSIGNMENT TO GET TO HEAVEN

There is no assignment to feel a certain way; no assignment to do the impossible and turn from sins. There's not even an assignment to be willing to turn from sin. Salvation is free, involving neither payment nor promise on our part. We are not our own salvation, nor are we a small part of our own atonement. If one chooses to call it an assignment, the only assignment doesn't have anything to do; it has a content to be believed: Jesus Christ, the Son of God, died for our sins, rose from the dead and promises everlasting life to anyone who trusts Him and Him alone for it.

In John 6:28, they ask Jesus the most important question of all time: "What must we do to do the works God requires?"

If there ever was a time for a complete answer and if there ever was a time when any doing of good or the giving up of the bad was in order, this is it. A prime opportunity has presented itself.

Jesus' answer: "The work of God is this: to believe in the One He has sent." There is no turning from sin, there is no baptism, no doing of a single piece of good. There is no feeling sorry or confession of sins. No penance, no promise.

John's gospel is evangelistic; its intent is to bring life to the reader. If repentance were necessary for salvation, we would expect to find the word sprinkled throughout the book, but we don't. John never uses "repent" one single time. The reason is obvious—repentance is inherent in the word "believe." When a person believes in Jesus, he has changed his mind.

Dr. Charles C. Ryrie, as usual, clarifies the issue: "Can a person repent without being saved? Yes; people do it all the time. A person may change his mind (repent) concerning a bad habit such as smoking and he may even break the habit as a result of his repentance. Yet, he remains unsaved." He continues, "Repentance for salvation involves a change of mind about Christ, so that whatever a person thought about Him before, he changes his mind and trusts Him to be his Savior. This is the only repentance (change of mind) that saves. Acts 17:30; II Peter 3:9; and Acts 20:21" (*Basic Theology,* p. 337).

Lewis Sperry Chafer wrote: "Sometimes it [repentance] is used as a synonym for faith because turning from every other confidence to trust Christ cannot happen without a change of mind. . . . Therefore the requirement for salvation is not repentance and faith. We see that in 150 cases, salvation is conditioned only upon believing" (Chafer, *Systematic Theology,* VII, p. 265).

TO PROCLAIM AND PROTECT

Paul wrote a polemic defending the gospel to the Galatians. In that book, the reader searches in vain for "repent" and it's as elusive as it is in John's book—"repent" isn't in Galatians any more than it is in John's gospel. The reader may search high and low for "repentance" connected with salvation in Romans; he won't find it there either.

Two New Testament books, one written to proclaim the gospel (John), the other to protect it (Galatians), and neither mention "repent." Their silence is saying something important.

Translating "repent" as "feel sorry for sin" causes problems when we plug that meaning into the New Testament sentences which use the word. In Acts 8:22 we read, "Repent therefore of this, your wickedness." If "repent" means "feel sorry for sin," then Luke wrote, "Therefore, feel sorry for this your sin sin." In II Cor. 12:21, Paul wrote, "And lest when I come again my God will humble me among you and that I shall bewail many which have sinned already and have not repented of the uncleanness." Therefore, he would be repeating himself by writing, ". . . and have not felt sorry for the sin uncleanness," i.e., "have not felt sorry for the sin sin." If repentance means to "feel sorry for sin," then the New Testament authors are writing, "Feel sorry for sin sin."

Yet, the notion persists that repentance has to do with more than a change of mind. For example, author Michael Green writes about doing evangelism: "Genuine repentance . . . means handing the keys of life to Christ and letting Him clear up the mess."

PERUSING REPENTANCE

What happened to "repent" happened to "peruse." In popular understanding both have come to mean what they do not mean. If I were to send you a magazine article and ask you to "peruse it," you'd understand me to mean, "Scan this article" or "Skim it without paying much attention to it." Yet, that's exactly the opposite of what "peruse" means. To "peruse" something is to "study and read something carefully, in detail" (Luntz, *Words that Work*). But, like repent, the word has been misused so often by so many people that the "skim it" definition is embedded in the English-speaking consciousness. Newspeak has embedded "repent" in our minds as "feel sorry for and turn from sin" to the point of encrustation. We need to repent of our traditional definition of repent!

CHAPTER FOUR

NEWSPEAK: "BELIEVE IS COMMIT, SUBMIT, OBEY, YIELD"

Newspeak takes the simplest of words and erects an edifice of complexity. Perhaps this is best seen by looking at what Newspeak did to "believe" and its associate, "faith." These are simple words, used in everyday conversation. In the case of "believe," John uses it ninety-nine times in his Gospel. Because of the abundant use of the word, it's important to get it right.

Newspeak has taken a massive toll on faith/believe, investing them with concepts which make salvation complex. From pulpits and pens, in the spoken and written word, we are told, "Faith includes obedience," that "Scripture often equates faith with obedience." Pulpits and pens load up the wagon when it comes to "saving faith," packing it with "hate sin and turn from it" (repentance), commitment, as well as a "self-denying, costly, and persistent following of Christ," and "obey God's word," all of which are deemed necessary.

HELL NEEDS TO GET READY

As proof, Oceanians ask us to read Jesus' statement to the Rich Young Ruler, "Sell all you have, give the proceeds to the poor, and follow Me." We are told this is the official, biblical definition of saving faith. But we need to be careful here. If this is the definitive statement of the gospel, then hell needs to get ready for an inundation of occupants because if the requirement to sell all, give all, and follow Christ is saving faith, then who is saved? The Oceanians must struggle with that question. And to answer it they must abandon a literal hermeneutic to interpret Jesus' statement because which pastor, evangelist, missionary, or layman has sold everything, given all the money to the poor, and followed Christ?

COMMIT OR BE WILLING TO COMMIT?

The Newspeakers, mollifying Jesus' stark staccato statement, add two words, "be willing to sell, give, and follow." In other words, so they themselves can enter the kingdom, the Newspeakers must deliteralize and retranslate Jesus' words, making them mean, "I'm just kidding; you don't have to do it; just be willing to do it."

But nowhere in the statement can we find "be willing." And the young rich one didn't take Jesus to mean, "Be willing; you don't have to really do it." He left saddened because he wouldn't do it. [Jesus was doing "pre-evangelism" with the man, showing him that he wasn't as dead solid perfect as he thought when it came to keeping the Law.]

We know that Jesus' statement to the Rich Young Ruler isn't the gospel because, in all the evangelistic sermons of the Apostles in the book of Acts, we see that they somehow forgot to include sell all, give all, and follow as prerequisites to one's entrance into glory. Not one gospel sermon that the Apostles preached includes the words, "Let me tell you how to be saved by telling you what we heard Jesus tell this rich fellow."

THE REFORMATION AND BELIEVE

Newspeakers tell us that the leaders of the Reformation understood biblical faith to include commitment, obedience, submission, and the yielding of one's life to Christ. But when we read the leaders of the Reformation, what do we find? "For, as regards justification, faith is something merely passive, bringing nothing of ours to the recovering of God's favor but receiving from Christ what we lack. We compare faith to a kind of vessel; for unless we come empty and with the mouth of our soul open to seek Christ's grace, we are not capable of receiving Christ" (Calvin).

It would appear that Calvin did not view faith as carrying a commitment component demanding obedience, submission, and the yielding of one's life to Christ. Faith's vessel, according to Calvin, was empty.

Another Reformation light wrote that faith was merely "receptivity." If we go back many hundreds of years prior to the Reformation, we note that Augustine said, "Faith is nothing else than to think with assent."

Saving faith is to be persuaded that something is true, trustworthy. It is no more and no less. Simple. Biblical saving faith is to be persuaded that Jesus Christ, the Son of God, died for your sins, rose from the dead, and promises everlasting life to anyone who trusts Him alone for that life. It is to trust Christ and Christ alone for one's eternal destiny. Simple.

THOSE PURITANS

When did Newspeak redefine "believe?" For the answer, we go back to the English Puritans who shifted faith from its passive sense of being persuaded that something is true to an active response which included the obedience, submission, commitment, and the yielding of the life to Christ.

Puritanism sounds ancient to us today, something way back there in the colonial days. It's true that Puritanism is no longer the powerful political force it once was, but its influence on American life has been both continuing and powerful. It was from the Puritans that Americans got their appreciation for hard work; it was Puritanism which influenced us to consider work a religious duty. For a long, long time, businesses in America shut down on Sunday, which, as sanctioned by the Puritans, was sacrosanct, as the "Christian Sabbath." Even the unbeliever had to observe it. [Never mind that it was Israel's Sabbath (Saturday) and never mind that neither America nor the church should ever be placed under the Mosaic Law, and never mind that the Mosaic Law as a way of life has been abolished, the Puritan influence shut business down.]

Blue laws came from the Puritan's influence on America. The first laws regulating public activities on Sundays were passed in colonial Virginia in the 1620s. Similar laws intended to keep the Sabbath holy were soon adopted elsewhere in America. Typically, all forms of trade or commerce were outlawed. No public entertainment or meetings were permitted, except for church services, which often included two-hour services in the morning and the afternoon. Travel on Sunday was banned, except for emergencies. It's always hard to be legalistic; there's always an exception in there somewhere.

The influence of blue laws didn't stop with the waning of the Puritans. We learn that "Individual states and communities implemented these laws throughout the late 1800s and the early 1900s. The State of Ohio implemented several blue laws, including one that prohibited alcohol sales on Sundays. Eventually, the Ohio government permitted alcohol sales after 1:00 PM on Sundays, a time when most church services had ended, and in the year 2000, Ohio Governor Bob Taft signed a law that permitted alcohol sales in sports arenas as early as 11:00 AM on Sundays." (*An Online Encyclopedia of Ohio History*)

Not only did the Puritans set in motion the plague of the blue laws, they infected "believe" with Newspeak. Lewellen writes: "In the Puritan era . . . there was a shift in the definition of saving faith. In the generations following the Reformation, some theologians subtly changed the Reformers' definition of faith from a passive receptivity to an active response on the part of the sinner, centered in the will and containing both commitment and obedience. . . . The idea that faith is an active commitment, including obedience, is the view of one strand of church history—English Puritanism—which is of course a powerful strand. One should not confuse that strand, however, with the "true church." Calvin disagreed with it; Lutheran theology has always opposed it; even today some Reformed theologians do not accept it" ("Lordship," pp. 58-59).

Thomas Watson (1620-1686), called "the most quotable and classic of the Puritans," wrote this: "He [Jesus] will never be a priest to intercede unless your heart is the throne where he sways his scepter. A true applying of Christ is when we so take him as a husband that we give up ourselves to him as Lord. Faith melts our will into God's. It runs at God's call. If God commands duty (though cross to flesh and blood) faith obeys. . . . Faith is not an idle grace; as it has an eye to see Christ, so it has a hand to work for him. It not only believes God's promise, but obeys his command." For Watson and the other Puritans, faith not only believed, faith obeyed.

AN ANGRY TOUR GUIDE

I was part of an excited tour group going to Israel. Before our departure from the States, our tour leader wanted to meet with us for instructions. We gathered in one designated room in the New York airport a few hours before the flight. He was well into his talk when two older ladies opened the door of the room and walked in. They were also part of the tour group, and the coming trip was the trip of a lifetime for them.

The tour leader stopped his talk, glared at the late-comers, as they paused to stare at him. That's when they said, "We're sorry we're late; have you said anything important?" At that, the self-absorbed guide lost his cool and began to lecture them and us on the importance of being on time from henceforth and forever more, world without end, amen.

We might ask the same thing: is this discussion of the nature of saving faith important or should it be the concern of cloistered, ivy-league academics only?

The definition of saving faith matters and matters vitally. Paul wrote in Galatians 1 that there is only one gospel that saves and if anyone doesn't declare it, he's to be anathema. There are "other gospels" out there, but only one saves. Which gospel it is, is a matter whose weight can't be overestimated.

Does God save a person by faith in Christ plus nothing or does He save a person through faith in Christ plus commitment, submission, obedience, and yieldedness? Does justification come through faith alone or faith plus? Is saving faith a faith with accompanying baggage or does it travel alone?

If one believes that faith is not to be alone, he has believed a gospel which does not save because there is only one which does, and that good news is the one which declares that the faith that saves is always alone.

SEA SICK

The faith-not-alone-group is cast upon a surging sea of subjectivity. Of what quality must the commitment, submission, obedience, and yieldedness be? The ultimate of each is martyrdom. Must it go that far or must there only be a willingness to go that far? How does one know how he would react before an authority demanding he reject Christ and burn incense to the Emperor or face the tigers in the

Coliseum tomorrow? If not to that point, then does a quality of 80% surrender hit the divine mark for entrance?

Another question emerges: how long must one commit, submit, surrender, yield, and obey? What if a person lives a surrendered life for twenty years, but the last six months of it does not, but sits at home, never going to church and wants nothing more to do with Christ and the Bible? Do the twenty faithful years trump the half year? Some may respond, "I that's what he does for six months, then he must not have been saved in the first place!" But consider Solomon.

Solomon's commitment to the Lord was not a life-long one. The man who wrote, "Trust in the Lord with all your heart and lean not on your own understanding; in all your ways acknowledge him, and he will make your paths straight," did not trust in the Lord with all his heart and did not acknowledge Him in all his ways. Instead, he broke God's standard of monogamy, married foreign women, and worshipped their idols. Solomon prayed the great prayer of I Kings 8:22-52 at the dedication of the Temple, yet he did not finish his life committed, obedient, submissive, and yielded.

Newspeak confuses people. The Oceanians will say things such as, "Faith alone justifies, but the faith that justifies is never alone." How can this be? How can justifying faith be alone and not alone? The Oceanians will say things such as, "Salvation is free, but it costs you everything." This too makes no sense; it's a sentence which contradicts itself. How can something which costs me nothing be costly to me? How can salvation be at one and the same time a gift for which I must work? It's akin to the statement that a person climbed eight flights of stairs to get to the basement.

VERBAL ALCHEMY

Newspeak gets confusing and complicated as in this statement: "Justification is based upon an imputed righteousness which completely delivers from the guilt and condemnation of sin. It is the only basis of our salvation. At the same time, we must recognize the necessity for repentance and submission to Christ as Lord in the application of that salvation."

Say what? One person, reading the above statement, said, "I have a headache." If justification completely delivers from the guilt and condemnation of sin and is the only basis of our salvation, then why are repentance from sin (i.e. turning from sin) and submission required? In one sentence, the justification is said to be complete and all that's needed. In the next sentence justification is said to be incomplete and more is needed for salvation. This is verbal alchemy.

PENANCE IS AS PENANCE DOES

Martin Luther fought against the system of penance because he knew that works were not necessary for justification. Whereas Protestants, based on their Reformation and biblical heritage, rightly reject the penance and sacramental systems, by making commitment, submission, obedience, surrender, and yieldedness faith's necessary companions, Protestants are only swapping one set of works for another, and once that's done, it's, "Move over Rome, we're here too!"

In Romans, Paul touts the "free gift" of the gospel. If salvation is free, how can a free gift cost the recipient commitment, obedience, and submission? The costs of salvation differ with each Oceanian who speaks or writes, thus adding more confusion to something as simple as the gospel. One might well ask, "What part of free gift don't you understand?"

MAXIMUM COMPLEXITY

Paul writes in Colossians about not allowing someone to take us away from the simplicity that is in Christ. Man, with his incurably religious bent, insists on taking the simple and making it ornate and complex. The Lord's Supper finds simplicity in the bread and the cup. Yet the religious man has transformed it into a ceremony complete with vestments, choreographed movements, pageantry, and vain repetitions. Not content with tampering with the bread and the cup, religious man complicates and thereby changes the gospel.

Listen to author Michael Green as he writes instructions concerning how to present the good news of the gospel: "The leader will want to make the way to Christ crystal clear and to allow the challenge of commitment to Christ to bite deep." We see immediately that Green has imported commitment into the gospel and not just any commitment, but one which has a deep bite.

To be "crystal clear," Green instructs the leader, "Tell the person: Repent, not just for your sins but for the great sin of proud rebellion and keeping your Lord at bay for so long." Then the leader is to bring the person to "Realize what He [Christ] has done through Bethlehem, Calvary, Easter, and Pentecost." One might wonder how the Day of Pentecost became part of the gospel message, but Green goes on to say that the leader must cause the person to "Reflect on the cost of discipleship. It is a commitment for life. It is going public. It is becoming number two to Jesus. It is going to church; it is working for God." We can see how complicated the simple gospel has gotten in such a presentation, not to mention confusing. Thrown into the salvational mix are "going public," "working for God," "going to church," and doing those things "for life." Keeping his alliterative skills in tact with a fourth "R," Green has one last step for the listener to do—he is to "Receive not just the truth in [his] head, but the Spirit of Jesus Himself into [his] heart and life." Repent. Realize. Reflect. Receive.

After going through the four steps, Green tells the leader, "You have explained the way . . . you now need to challenge each of them publicly to declare his hand just as Jesus did. . . ."

(*Evangelsim Through the Local Church*, pp. 441-442) But did Jesus demand that people declare themselves publicly? He told Nicodmus that he must be born again in the dead of night, privately. He even dismissed His disciples so that He could speak to the woman at the well privately.

Green makes sure that the one witnessing understands that "[you the evangelist are to] ask who will join you in a prayer of commitment then and there. It is truly evangelism which issues in a life that is changed from going my way to going Christ's way."

But did Paul think so? What Green is talking about is a Romans 12:1-2 decision and what he's doing is importing "presenting oneself a living sacrifice" into the gospel. But we can see the fallacy of such thinking when we realize that the people to whom Paul is writing that command are believers whose faith people are talking about "all over the world" (Romans 1:6-8). They are already saved and in Christ. If a Romans 12:1-2 commitment to Christ is necessary for salvation, why is Paul commanding these who are already believers and whose faith is being talked about all over the world to make such a commitment? Wouldn't they have had to do so in order to be saved?

That was a long gospel haul with its four steps, and after it's all said and done, works are converging all over from the north, south, east, and west, creating a perfect storm, leaving the convert to wonder if he'll be able to endure church all his life and work for God all his life. And what's this about having to know about Pentecost and having to receive the Spirit of Jesus? How did those things get in there? Was part of Paul's message to the gentiles that they know of the Day of Pentecost?

Green goes so far as to quote Pope Paul VI so that "We may learn from our Catholic brethren what is truly evangelism." He calls the Roman Catholic Church "the most respectable of all denominations." Yet it is Roman Catholicism which is obese with works. Roman Catholicism is a veritable feast of works as it decries justification by faith alone and always has. Its bloody tooth and claw persecution of grace has been writ large in one history book after another. Yet, Green finds their evangelism commendable and their institution the most respected.

Green fills his evangelism with "commit" and summarizes it all by writing under four headings, "There is something to admit, there is something to believe, there is something to consider, and there is something to do."

There's no simplicity in that Newspeak. To complicate the gospel is to change it.

This is why Newspeak is devastating. As the words of the Newspeak roll off tongue and press, as Newspeak pours forth it's sermons, teaches its Sunday school classes, and writes its books, the gospel lies in a wreckage of works. Such a gospel, glutted by works, is gutted of saving truth.

CHAPTER FIVE

NEWSPEAK: "JUSTIFIED MEANS GUILTY UNTIL PROVEN RIGHTEOUS"

Justification with its thirteen letters is the longest of the five most important words in Christianity. The rescue of this word from Newspeak changed Europe, England, and influenced America. Would it be too much of a stretch to say that the meaning of justification is inextricably bound up with Western Civilization? Bildad, one of those who dialogued with Job, asked an important question: "How can a man be justified with God?" (Job 25:4) The answer to that question is a great divide. To understand the Bible's answer, it's important to see what justification is not.

Justification by faith alone means that man is not put right before God by any past, present, or future achievement on his part. Justification is not a process; it's an act. Justification is not won or earned over time. It has nothing to do with a person's gradual goodness gained by giving up sins or by his disciplined practice of various virtues.

WHAT JUSTIFICATION IS

The standard theological definition of justification is, "The judicial decree of God whereby the sinner is declared righteous by faith in Christ." "To stand justified" is to be credited positionally with the very righteousness of Christ.

It's not a decree which we earn or deserve; it is a decree issued by God on the sinner's behalf upon faith in Christ, paying no attention to the sinner's merit or demerit. The decree has only to do with grace alone through faith alone in Christ alone. God doesn't grant the decree based on a person's good acts in the past, those he's presently doing, or will do in the future. That's why David called justification a "blessing" (Psalm 32:1-2).

GOOD QUESTION, WRONG ANSWER

Ask most believers, "Are you guilty?" The majority would answer with a loud, "Yes!" Such is the confusion abounding today, a confusion based upon an ignorance of their justified state and perhaps a desire to appear humble. But Christianity isn't a pose or a pretend. (Leave phoniness to the religionists.) God's decree of justification pronounces the believer, "Not guilty," and is a declaration that God has credited to him the righteousness of Christ. Justification is a positive concept in that the righteousness of Christ has been credited to the believer's account on the basis of faith alone. Christ's work on the cross achieved a great negative, the taking away of sins for the believer and accomplished a positive—the crediting of His righteousness to the forgiven sinner.

When God looks at the believer, He sees the righteousness of His Son; He has credited a perfect righteous standing to the believer apart from any good things the sinner has done and apart from any bad things the sinner has sworn off and given up or is willing to swear off and give up.

WHAT THE BIBLE SAYS

Genesis 15:6: "And Abraham believed God and it was counted to him for righteousness."

Romans 4:5-6: "But to the one who does not work, but believes in the one who justifies the ungodly, his faith is reckoned as righteousness just as also David says about the blessing of the man to whom God reckons righteousness apart from works."

Romans 3:8: "For we maintain that a man is justified by faith apart from the works of the Law."

Philippians 3:9: "and be found in him, not having a righteousness of my own that comes from the law, but that which is through faith in Christ—the righteousness that comes from God and is by faith."

Romans 10:3: "Christ is the end of the law so that there may be righteousness for everyone who believes."

Romans 5:17, 19: "For if, by the trespass of the one man, death reigned through that one and, how much more will those who receive God's abundant provision of grace and of the gift of righteousness reign in life through the one man, Jesus Christ," and "For just as through the disobedience of the one man the many were made sinners, so also through the obedience of the one man the many will be made righteous."

Notice the vocabulary used with justification in those statements: "to the one who does not work . . . his faith is counted as righteousness," "apart from works," "not having my own righteousness," "the righteousness which comes from God and is by faith," "the gift of righteousness," and "through the obedience of one man." Those Scriptures add up to a strong phalanx marshaling their forces to say, "Christ's righteousness is a free gift."

SAUL THE WORKER MAN

Saul was a law-doer to the core of his being. He was a Pharisee devoted to the Mosaic Law as the basis for acceptance before

God. Yet, by divine revelation he came to know that he was justified by faith and that God had announced the verdict "Not guilty" for him just as He does for every one who trusts Christ alone. God had shown him that his justification didn't grow with the practice of good works, nor did it lessen when the believer becomes less righteous. The declaration is not based on our growing inward holiness. Paul writes in Romans 3:24 that the believer is justified "without a cause," that is, without a cause in himself. There is no requirement on our part except faith.

The only way the believer can lose the righteousness of Christ is if Christ's own righteousness were to fail. The getting of this righteousness doesn't involve a moral change on our part; as we see in Romans 3:24, it is without a cause in us. As Lewis Sperry Chafer said, "As long as Christ's righteousness endures, the believer's endures." The believer is said to be "in Christ" at the moment he trusts Christ. That is his position and legal standing before God. Positionally, in Christ, the believer will never become more positionally and legally righteous before God than he was the day he trusted Christ.

THE HOWLING OF THE WOLVES

Newspeak has kicked up the sand of confusion all around justification and the first kickers are those we've already met, the Church Fathers. Paul warned the Ephesian elders that wolves would teach perversions of the truth, drawing away disciples after them. "Keep watch over yourselves and all the flock of which the Holy Spirit has made you overseers. Be shepherds of the church of God, which he bought with his own blood. I know that after I leave, savage wolves will come in among you and will not spare the flock. Even from your own number men will arise and distort the truth in order to draw away disciples after them" (Acts 20:28-30). They came, they taught, they led astray.

Their teaching on justification was 180 degrees from Paul's. Clement wrote, "We should clothe ourselves with concord, being humble, self-controlled, far removed from all gossiping and slandering, and justified by our deeds, not by words" (ch. 30:3). Clement says that Abraham earned the birth of Isaac: "Because of [Abraham's] faith and hospitality a son was granted to him in his old age" (ch. 10:7).

On the other hand, Clement wrote: "And we, therefore . . . are not justified of ourselves or by our wisdom or insight or religious devotion or the holy deeds we have done from the heart, but by that faith by which almighty God has justified all men from the very beginning" (ch. 32:4).

Which is it? On the one hand it's faith alone; no, on the other hand it's, "[we are] justified by our deeds. . ."

Justin, confused, wrote: "Those who are found not living as he taught should know that they are not really Christians, even if his teachings are on their lips, for he said that not those who merely profess but those who also do the works will be saved" (*The First Apology of Justin*, ch. 16). He also wrote, "Each man goes to everlasting punishment or salvation according to the value of his actions" (*The First Apology of Justin*, ch. 7). He went on: "The matters of our religion lie in works, not in words" (*Hortatory Address to the Greeks*, ch. 35).

Iraneus, also a Newspeaker, says, "But to the righteous and holy, and those who have kept his commandments and have remained in his love . . . he will by his grace give life incorrupt, and will clothe them with eternal glory" (*Against Heresies*, Bk. IV, ch. XIII).

Yet, the same author picked up his quill and wrote, "No one, indeed while placed out of reach of our Lord's benefits, has power to procure for himself the means of salvation. So the more we receive His grace, the more we should love Him" (*Against Heresies*, Bk. IV, ch. XIII).

Contradictions abound. On the one hand they say, "God will, by His grace, give life to those who have kept his commandments and have remained in His love," and on the other they say, "Yet no one has the power to procure for himself the means of salvation"; then they write, "Yet it is to those who have kept the commandments that He will give life."

Shepherds are to teach the sheep, not confuse them. The Church Fathers are confusing because they are doing what Paul commanded should not be done—mixing works into grace.

THE CHURCH FATHERS EMBEDDED

The theology of the Church Fathers is embedded in Roman Catholicism.

Roman Catholic doctrine denies justification by faith alone and says:

> If any one saith, that by faith alone the impious is justified; in such wise as to mean, that nothing else is required to cooperate in order to the obtaining of the grace of Justification, and that it is not in any way necessary, that he be prepared and disposed by the movement of his own will; let him be anathema (Council of Trent, *Canons on Justification*, Canon 9).

> If any one saith, that man is truly absolved from his sins and justified, because he assuredly believed himself absolved and justified; or, that no one is truly justified but he who believes himself justified; and that, by this faith alone, absolution and justification are effected; let him be anathema (Canon 14).

The reader may wonder what's necessary, then, in addition to faith? Rome's answer is:

Of the acts to be performed by Catholics for justification, baptism is the first requirement:

> . . . Baptism is the first and chief sacrament of forgiveness of sins because it unites us with Christ, who died for our sins and rose for our justification, so that "we too might walk in newness of life" (*Catechism of the Catholic Church*, par. 977).

> Justification has been merited for us by the Passion of Christ. It is granted us through Baptism. It conforms us to the righteousness of God, who justifies us. It has for its goal the glory of God and of Christ, and the gift of eternal life. It is the most excellent work of God's mercy (*CCC*, par. 2020).

Baptism is only the starting point. There's more: However, according to Roman Catholicism even faith and baptism aren't sufficient in themselves for you to be saved. It says that baptism is only the first sacrament of forgiveness. Good works, according to Roman Catholicism, are also required and are rewarded with going to heaven:

> We can therefore hope in the glory of heaven promised by God to those who love him and do his will. In every circumstance, each one of us should hope, with the grace of God, to persevere 'to the end' and to obtain the joy of heaven, as God's eternal reward for the good works accomplished with the grace of Christ. (*CCC*, par. 1821).

In a direct contradiction to the definition of grace, we read in the Catechism of the Catholic Church (*CCC*), par. 2010, "Moved by the Holy Spirit and by charity, we can then merit for ourselves and for others the graces needed for our sanctification."

Here we see that, although the word "graces" is used, it is said, ". . .we can then merit for ourselves and for others the graces needed for our sanctification." In such a statement, grace as "unmerited favor" is expelled and man's meriting of grace has taken its place. Grace merited is not grace. Such is the confusion and contradiction of Newspeak.

According to the embedded theology, once the sinner is justified, he must be careful lest he lose his position. So says Roman Catholic theology: "Christ instituted the sacrament of Penance for all sinful members of his Church: above all for those who, since Baptism, have fallen into grave sin, and have thus lost their baptismal grace and wounded ecclesial communion. It is to them that the sacrament of Penance offers a new possibility to convert and to recover the grace of justification." The Fathers of the Church present this sacrament as "the second plank (of salvation) after the shipwreck which is the loss of grace" (CCC, par. 1446).

In the Roman system, there come times when the justified sinner must recover his former justified state and the priest stands ready to make the various assignments necessary for the retrieving of the justification lost. Justification becomes an on-again-off-again matter wherein the sinner is guilty (again) and must prove himself righteous (again) by various works (again). The works run the gamut from prayer, saying the rosary, reading the Scripture, saying an assigned number of "Our Fathers" or "Hail Marys," doing good works, fasting, and other such things. Works. Works. Works.

TRUTH TO THE RESCUE

However, there is no need for concern because there's no sin or sins which can cause the justified believer to revert to the unjustified sinner. Romans 8:38-39: "For I am convinced that neither death nor life, neither angels nor demons, neither the present nor the future, nor any powers, neither height nor depth, nor anything else in all creation, will be able to separate us from the love of God that is in Christ Jesus our Lord." The "things present," the "things future" would include present and future sins, none of which will be able to separate us from our once and forever justification.

We have Jesus' word that our justification certificate is a forever decree:

John 6:35: "I am the bread of life. He who comes to me will never go hungry, and he who believes in me will never be thirsty."

John 6:37: "All that the Father gives me will come to me, and whoever comes to me I will never drive away."

John 6:39: "And this is the will of him who sent me, that I shall lose none of all that he has given me, but raise them up at the last day."

John 4:14: ". . . but whoever drinks the water I give him will never thirst. Indeed, the water I give him will become in him a spring of water welling up to eternal life."

John 10:28: "I give them eternal life, and they shall never perish; no one can snatch them out of my hand."

The no ones, the nones, and the nevers add up to a strong fortress built around a securely justified believer.

The Corinthian believers are a case study in carnality run amok in the church. Paul has to deal with severe abuses at the Lord's supper, rampant divisions, immorality, tongues gone wild, divorces, and doctrinal problems such as the infiltration of pagan philosophy, to name some.

Paul wrote that he couldn't talk to them as spiritual, but only as carnal believers, operating in the flesh, indistinguishable from unbelievers (I Cor. 3). Yet, in I Cor. 6:11, Paul describes them this way: "Such were some of you, but you were washed. But you were sanctified. But you were justified in the name of the Lord Jesus, and in the Spirit of our God."

Carnal, in sin, the various sin natures on a rampant carnage, all combining to produce believers indistinguishable to the human eye from the unbeliever, yet, he says, "you were washed," "you were sanctified," and "you were justified." The washing, the sanctification, and the justification all have one thing in common: they cannot be taken away since God promises in Romans 11:29, "For the gifts and the calling of God are irrevocable."

Paul tells the reader that justification, the crediting of the believer's account with the righteousness of Christ, is a gift in Romans 5:16-18: "The gift is not as through one who sinned: for the judgment came by one to condemnation, but the free gift came of many trespasses to justification. For if by the trespass of the one, death reigned through the one; so much more will those who receive the abundance of grace and of the gift of righteousness reign in life through the one, Jesus Christ. Therefore as by the offence of one judgment came upon all men to condemnation; even so by the righteousness of one the free gift came upon all men unto justification of life."

GOING HOME, JUSTIFIED

In Luke 18:14, Jesus pronounced the sinner justified at that time, an immediate justification apart from works. There was no "let's-wait-and-see-if-he-earns-it" attitude. His justification was not something he worked toward, but something as a present tense decree in his life right then and there, before he went home. The Pharisee was trying to work toward his justification, something he would never achieve, for as Paul wrote: "Because by the works of the law, no flesh will be justified in his sight. For through the law comes the knowledge of sin." Trying to adjust to the righteous demands of the law doesn't justify anyone; it makes them realize their inherent, everyday practice of and slavery to sin.

THE ANCIENT PICKPOCKETS

With Newspeak, one cannot know if he's justified or not. "Have I done enough for long enough" and "Has the good been good enough," are ever-harassing questions.

But in the language of Newspeak, a person justified has to earn it and if he has to earn it, then it's possible that it can be unearned and lost, so the only thought he can think using Newspeak is that justified means guilty until proven righteous by a lifetime prescription of works.

Newspeak picks the believer's pocket, robbing him of assurance, the assurance of a once-for-all decree which legally certifies that God has credited him with the righteousness of Christ and that he stands before God positionally righteous forever.

CHAPTER SIX

THE AUGEAN STABLES

There are many myths about Hercules, the son of Zeus and a mortal. One of the most famous stories about Hercules concerns his Twelve Labors, assigned to him by the god Apollo after Hercules went crazy and murdered his own family. None of these labors, assigned by Apollo to atone for the murders, were believed to be possible for anyone to complete. Wherever we look in history, whatever religion it is, people naturally think that they are their own atonement.

The fifth of those Twelve Labors was the cleaning of the Augean Stables. King Augeas was cheap, and while he was rich enough to own thousands of cows, bulls, goats, horses, and sheep, he had never been willing to pay for the services of someone to clean the stables. The assignment: Hercules was to clean the Augean stables in one day.

Impossible. The difficulty of such a thing has become a proverbial statement. ("Augean stables" is now synonymous with "Herculean task," which is itself the equivalent of saying that something is all but humanly impossible.)

When Hercules went to Augeas, he offered to clean the stables in one day if the king would give him a tenth his finest livestock. The king agreed and Hercules took the ruler's son as a witness.

First, Hercules tore a big opening in the wall where the stables were, then he made an opening on the opposite side of the cattle yard. He dug trenches to two rivers which flowed nearby. The Greek hero next turned the flow of the rivers, the Alpheius and the Peneius into the yard; the rivers rushed through the stables, causing the mess to flow out the opening in the other side. The stables were clean; Hercules had won the day.

When it comes to the subject of reclaiming the five important words in Christianity, it's like cleaning the Augean stables because Newspeak has created a theological mess in our minds.

Christian families and churches aren't grounding people in the gospel. This is borne out by the fact that although the Bible presents the free grace way of salvation and the Koran and the Book of Mormon present works ways of salvation, 61% of those who say they are Christians agree that all three books are saying the same thing, or they don't know whether they are or not.

We're not to wring our hands and say, "Woe is us;" instead we are to make disciples grounded in the gospel. Grace-oriented discipleship can clean the Augean Stables.

Cleaning the stables starts at the top with male leadership. The leaders of the church are to be mature men, grounded in the gospel. Titus 1: "He [an elder] must hold firmly to the trustworthy message as it has been taught, so that he can encourage others by sound doctrine and refute those who oppose it."

With no deviation, the leadership is to hold the message as it has been taught. No slight modifications, no changes in the message to make it more relevant, to make it attractive to the unbeliever, to increase attendance, but these men are to give the good news as Christ and the Apostles taught it. This command walks parallel to Paul's command to Timothy to "guard the gospel." That guarding should be with one's life. If one of the leaders of the church is not willing to lose his position for the sake of the gospel, then he shouldn't be leading the church.

THE PROBLEM WITH HIGH SCHOOL COACHES

When asked, "What was your favorite subject in school," history is rarely the answer. The reason for this is because most of the history teachers are coaches and coaches are more interested in X's, O's, and winning the next game. If a history teacher has no passion for the past, his students will find it difficult to get excited about The War Between the States.

I had a professor of Latin and Greek Terminology who was so in love with words and their origins, that he gave his son a dictionary for Christmas. No kidding. Because of his passion for words, those in his classes built huge vocabularies that semester, vocabularies which have stayed with them all their lives. If the leaders of a church aren't excited about the grace of God, the church won't care either. We see Paul's passion throbbing in statements such as, "Woe is me if I preach not the gospel" and "I become all things to all men that I might win some." What is it that excites your pastor, elders and deacons? Are they dominated by a magnificent obsession with grace? If they're not, they're in the wrong position.

Cleaning the stables involves a clear and consistent pulpit. It's not to be one Sunday, the gospel becomes this, and the next Sunday, the gospel transforms into that. It's not to be one Sunday a visiting speaker says, "Believe in Jesus, feel sorry for, and turn from your sins," and the regular pastor-teacher says, "Faith alone." It's not to be permitted that one speaker has four steps and another five or six for salvation. If the pulpit is confused, the people will be confused, as the Old Testament says, "Like priest, like people." The rivers of the pure waters of grace must then cascade from the pulpit into every educational endeavor of the church.

HERE'S THE QUARTERLY, NOW ENTER THE LIONS' DEN

Cleaning the stables involves Sunday School teachers. You've got to hand it to Home Depot. That corporation knows about getting its message to children at the earliest ages; the only problem is that it's a deadly message they're disseminating because Home Depot is sponsoring a children's booth with children's workshops at Gay Pride Festivals. I say you've got to hand it to them because they know that the next generation is the important one.

Israel was to have that attitude, as we learn from Deuteronomy 6: "These commandments that I give you today are to be upon your hearts. Impress them on your children. Talk about them when you sit at home and when you walk along the road, when you lie down and when you get up (i. e. in life settings). Tie them as symbols on your hands and bind them on your foreheads. Write them on the door frames of your houses and on your gates." This is a total grace saturation by trained teachers who are not simply handed a quarterly and pointed to the den of young lions prowling the middle school boys Sunday school class. The five Bible words with their Bible definitions and their theology, must consistently be taught and shown in their biblical contexts.

GET GRACE OUT OF THE PEW

Cleaning the stables involves both youth and adults trained in and given opportunities for free grace evangelism. This would involve training in the classroom and on-the-task training such as the trainee's observing a "trainer/coach" in the actual witnessing. The model is Christ and His Word. We see Jesus doing this in the training of the Twelve. He taught them; then He placed them in His walking classroom in which they encountered all kinds of uncomfortable situations in a fallen world. They learned from Him when they saw His interaction with people in real time, interaction full of grace and full of truth. Then, just before the Ascension, He commanded them to start walking and go into all the world with the gospel and make disciples.

READ GRACE

Cleaning the stables involves the printed page. Deuteronomy 6: "Write them on the door frames of your houses and on your gates." This would include books, periodicals, and articles from sources inside and outside of the member's church which present a consistent free grace message. The home in which I grew up had grace literature piled high. We referred to it as our mother's "stack." It was from that literature that I came to understand that tithing is not for the believer today. I remember where I was when I was reading about grace-giving from "the stack."

GRACE ALERTS

Cleaning the stables involves the leadership of the church alerting the congregation to false gospels. Paul warned the Galatians (Gal. 1:6-9) and the elders at Ephesus (Acts 28) concerning present and future attacks on free grace. In Titus, the elders are to be men who can refute false gospels. Once alerted by the leadership, parents do not expose their children to those teaching a false gospel; they don't buy the books; they do not watch the DVDs; they do not send their children to the camps, the Sunday school classes, or that VBS. As wise stewards, they support free grace ministries with their attendance and their wallets.

THINK SMALL

Cleaning the stables involves getting up close. As the saying goes, "You impress people from afar. You impact people up close." Small discipleship groups, small study groups, easily surface both questions and confusion in people's minds. People will express themselves more readily in a small setting rather than in an auditorium. We must allow them to irrigate our small group meetings with questions. We must think small and be willing to meet with people in little groups, up close and personal, in order to get their questions and confusion into the open.

LET ME ENTERTAIN YOU?

How did the Apostles make disciples? They established churches. To clean the stables, churches aren't to be entertainment centers, but encouraging, grace-oriented training centers in which people grow in grace. (There's a difference between being interesting and being entertaining.) The world will always entertain better, but the world will never ground anyone in grace, so attendance at a grace-oriented church which trains believers in grace is a necessity whether that church has an up-to-date nursery or not.

This brings us to Paul and his command to Timothy which parallels what we've seen and is, again, the justification for the all of the above. I Timothy 2:2: "And the things you have heard me say in the presence of many witnesses entrust to reliable men who will also be qualified to teach others."

How do you ground people in the gospel? Through academic (teaching) and experiential (real life witnessing situations) saturation in grace.

THINK IN THE NEGATIVE

Cleaning the stables involves thinking negatively. When Paul came to define salvation by grace alone, he helped his readers to understand what grace is by teaching them what it isn't. He did not let his readers define grace; he told them what it is and what it is not. In Ephesians 2:8-9, he writes, "For it is by grace you have been saved, through faith—and this not from yourselves, it is the gift of God—not by works, so that no one can boast."

In II Timothy 2:9, he wrote, ". . . who has saved us and called us with a holy calling, not according to our works, but according to His own purpose and grace which was granted us in Christ Jesus from all eternity . . ."

In Titus 3:5 he says, "He saved us, not because of righteous things we had done, but because of his mercy. He saved us through the washing of rebirth and renewal by the Holy Spirit . . ." In I Corinthians 1:17 Paul points out one specific work which is not a part of the gospel when he writes, "For Christ did not send me to baptize, but to preach the gospel . . ."

We read the this-is-what-grace-isn't-clarifications in Romans and Galatians:

> Romans 3:27-28: "Where, then, is boasting? It is excluded. On what principle? On that of observing the law? No, but on that of faith."

> Galatians 3:11: "Clearly no one is justified before God by the law. . ."

This isn't a Pauline phenomena of negativity only. John writes, "Yet to all who received him, to those who believed in his name, he gave the right to become children of God—children born not of natural descent, nor of human decision or a husband's will, but born of God" (John 1:12-13).

We see from these references that the New Testament authors aren't content to let the reader define grace. Today, the assumption that a person can accurately define grace is both faulty and dangerous because of the Newspeak implant.

LIGHT AT THE BACK DOOR

A lady from another church once listened attentively to a Bible study I taught over an eight-week period on Galatians. Hundreds of times we made the trek from the Law of Mt. Sinai to the grace of Calvary, always to re-enforce the same message: the Mosaic Law is not, and never was the means of salvation, the Mosaic Law is not the way of life for the believer today; the Mosaic Law is gone, over and done with, abolished (II Cor. 3; Heb. 7).

On the last night of the study, she stopped as she was leaving the church to tell me how much she had enjoyed and benefited from it. She was very kind and gracious in her remarks, and in addition to my telling her that I'd like to have her glowing comments notarized, I said, "Yes, it's important for us to know that the Law of Moses can't save us and isn't our way of life once we're saved."

Immediately, her face reflected the fact that some new thought had created a brain storm. She asked, "Moses? Moses-Moses? Mosaic Law? That Moses?"

Since I had no idea what she was talking about I asked what she meant.

What had happened was that she'd put together something she'd never seen before until that back door, Damascus Road experience. She told me that now she understood, whereas in all the eight weeks, right up until that night, right then at the door, saying good-bye, she'd thought that when I talked about the Mosaic Law, I was talking about a mosaic of laws, a patchwork of laws pieced together from the ancient world. So much for my pedagogical skills!

It was also a Damascus Road experience for me—I assumed that everyone knew what I was talking about when I referenced the Mosaic Law. She didn't, and I've often wondered that, had she not stopped and talked at the door, if she ever would have understood. It was an eight-week experience of my talking right past her, seeing her listening intently, and my not knowing she was, at every moment, thinking I was saying what I was not saying.

REAGAN vs. MONDALE: A REVELATION

Back in the presidential election of the 1980s, on a lark, I decided to spend the election day working for CBS News doing exit polling. After being trained as to what to ask and how to ask it, armed with clipboard and pen, I spent the day asking people exiting from the polls various questions concerning for whom they cast their ballot and why. It turned out to be an eye-opening day.

It was the election of Reagan against Mondale, or as some would say, Mr. Conservative versus Mr. Liberal, and that was where one of our CBS-assigned questions entered the picture. Over and over again, I was to ask and record the answer to the question, "Do you consider yourself a conservative or a liberal?" An overwhelming percentage of the respondents answered, "Conservative." It was the most consistently given answer by far that day.

The follow-up question was, "For whom did you vote?" Surprisingly, many of the "conservatives" would respond, "Mondale." It happened many times before I began to realize that they didn't understand the meaning of the word. It was not a case of one or two people answering that way, but Mondale voters were consistently answering in such a fashion, rendering the terms meaningless.

SURVEY SAYS

Fast forward over the years, and, still having a fondness for surveys, I'm sitting at a table surveying people concerning their spiritual viewpoints during our church's fall festival, an open house for the community. The survey is a diagnostic tool which will lead the questioner to give the gospel at the conclusion of the survey. No tricky manipulations are involved, no canned approaches, because the one asking the questions is listening and interacting with the person's answers and always secures the person's permission to tell him about Christ.

EVERYBODY "JUST KNOWS"

When I asked every one being interviewed, "What does grace mean," their answers were all over the map. People either had no idea or they hazarded guesses, all the way from, "What you say before you eat," to "An inner quality of style," to "I've heard the word all my life, but I don't know." Their answers weren't given with certainty, but with hesitancy, as when their answer would be phrased as a question. I found that the definition was unknown to the educated as well as the uneducated; the word was beyond their grasp.

What's happening is that people in our churches are sitting in the pew Sunday after Sunday, hearing grace thrown around the auditorium and singing songs about how amazing it is, but we're leaving it up to them to define it, and they're coming up with the wrong definitions. Everybody doesn't "just know."

We must define it, but then we don't kill it later with conditions, strings, vows, promises to God to do better and try harder. We must not ask them to turn from their sins or that they hand their lives over to the Lord to be saved.

EVERYBODY HAS AND IS A STORY

Cleaning the stables involves story-telling. Besides carefully crafting our language to be precise with the Bible's definition, we can become what the Bible is—a repository of grace stories. There's nothing like telling the stories of grace. God filled His Book with them. This is especially applicable today because we live in a story-soaked society. People are accustomed to reading stories as they sit in airports (novels); they're accustomed to sitting in front of their television sets watching stories. They spend billions to let stories entertain them in movie theaters. They buy and read story books to their children. Even in sports, they like a story line. The teams clashing next Sunday may be the underdog David against the highly favored Goliath, or a Cinderella story of one team's rise from worst to first.

And in the telling of the stories, we can show what grace is and what it's not. In John 4, when we read the story of the woman at the well, a sinful outcast if ever there was one, we should be specific and point out, not only what John records about the freeness of the gift of salvation, but also that Jesus, in saving her, didn't make her promise that she would immediately separate from the man who was not her husband. Unless we point to the fact of what Jesus did not demand of her, we leave the hearer to his own observational skills.

Grace is the baseline in our Bible dictionary. Once a person understands that one word, then all the others, repent, finished, justified, and believe, logically fall into place in grace.

Once a person has understood grace and its implications, he has the river to clean the Augean Stables. This, then, will make Newspeak, like Latin, one more dead language.

BIBLIOGRAPHY

Aquinas, Thomas. *Summa Theologia*. New York: Benzinger Brothers, 1948.

Bainton, Roland H. *Here I Stand: A Life of Martin Luther*. Peabody, MA: Hendrickson Publishers Marketing, 1950.

Bing, Charles C. *Lordship Salvation: A Biblical Evaluation and Response*. GraceLife Edition. Burleson, TX: GraceLife Ministries, 1992.

Boettner, Loraine. *Roman Catholicism*. Philippsburg, NJ: The Presbyterian and Reformed Publishing Co., 1962.

Cairnes, Earle E. *Christianity through the Centuries*. Grand Rapids: Zondervan, 1954.

Chafer, Lewis Sperry. *Grace: An Exposition of God's Marvelous Gift*. Grand Rapids: Kregel Publications, 1995.

_____. *Systematic Theology*. Dallas: Dallas Theological Seminary, 1948.

Dante, Alighieri. *Inferno*. New York: Random House, 1970.

Green, Michael. *Evangelism through the Local Church*. Nashville: Oliver-Nelson Books, 1992.

Gunther, Peter F. *A Frank Boreham Treasury: Favorite Bible Texts that have Changed Lives*. Chicago: Moody Press, 1984.

Hixson, J. B. *Getting the Gospel Wrong*. N.p.: Xulon Press, 2008.

Iranaeus. *Against Heresies*. Roberts and Donaldson, editors. Ex
    Fontibus Company.
Lewellen, Thomas G. "Has Lordship Salvation Been Taught
    throughout Church History?" *Bibliotheca Sacra* 147
    (January 1990): 54-68.
Luntz, Frank. *Words that Work*. New York: Hyperion, 2007.
Lybrand, Fred R. *Back to Faith*. N.p.: Xulon Press, 2009.
Orwell, George. *1984*. New York: Signet Classic, 1950.
Ryrie, Charles C. *Basic Theology*. Chicago: Moody Press. 1999.
Stegall, Thomas L. *The Gospel of the Christ*. Milwaukee: Grace
    Gospel Press, 2009.
Sungenis, Robert A. *Not by Faith Alone: The Biblical Evidence
    for the Catholic Doctrine of Justification*. Goleta, CA:
    Queenship Publishing Co., 1997.
Torrance, Thomas F. *The Doctrine of Grace in the Apostolic
    Fathers*. Eugene, OR: Wipf and Stock Publishers, 1948.
Watson, Thomas. *The Godly Man's Picture*. Carlisle, PA: The
    Banner of Truth Trust, 1992.

SUBJECT & PERSON INDEX

SCRIPTURE INDEX

CPSIA information can be obtained at www.ICGtesting.com
Printed in the USA
BVOW071547071212

307519BV00001B/28/P